Lament for Jerusalem

Lament for Jerusalem

Yasmine Zahran

GILGAMESH
PUBLISHING LTD

Lament for Jerusalem

Published by Gilgamesh Publishing in 2011
Email: info@gilgamesh-publishing.co.uk
www.gilgamesh-publishing.co.uk

ISBN 978-1-908531-02-5

© Yasmine Zahran 2011

Printed and bound by CPI (UK) Ltd, Croydon, CR0 4YY

All rights are reserved. No part of this publication
may be reproduced, stored in a retrieval system or transmitted in any form or
by any means, electronic, mechanical, photographic or otherwise, without
prior permission of the copyright holder.

CIP Data: A catalogue for this book is
available from the British Library

To Jerusalem

occupied, mutilated and forced to change its identity, and for her children massacred at Mamilla in 614 who "only God knows their names"[1]

This lament is for her past and present misfortune

---

[1] A Greek inscription in a rock cut burial cave discovered in Mamilla with an adjoining chapel used for the burial of the victims of 614, demolished by the Israelis.

TABLE OF CONTENTS

Preface by Professor Robert Hoyland	9
Author's Note	11
Prologue: Repeated Cycles?	13

THE EMPIRE OF THE RISING SUN

Chapter I – Kisra II (Parviz) Avenger and Destroyer	17
Chapter II – The Great War: Persian Supremacy	32
Chapter III – The Sack of Jerusalem	42
The Lament of Sophronius	65
Chapter IV – The Feast of the Cross	69

THE EMPIRE OF THE SETTING MOON

Chapter V – Heraclius: The First Crusader	83
Chapter VI – The Great War: The Roman Counter-offensive	96
Chapter VII – Two Sirens: Shirin and Martina	111
Chapter VIII – The Arabian Factor in the War	123
Epilogue	135
Bibliography	137

Preface

The capture of Jerusalem in AD 614 was a highly traumatic affair for the Christian world, with tens of thousands of the faithful slaughtered, numerous churches razed, and the city's patriarch and the Holy Cross removed to Persia. The end came swiftly. Having taken Damascus in the autumn of 613, the Persians then entered Palestine, encountering no resistance as they advanced via Tiberias, Caesarea and along the coast. Striking inland, they reached Jerusalem in the early summer of 614 and, within a month, they had besieged and sacked it and carried off its treasures. Christian onlookers smote their faces, strewed ashes on their heads and tore their hair, sobbing and lamenting, as they watched the bastion of Christendom being devoured by flames. Jews gave ecstatic praise to Yahweh who had seemingly delivered them from foreign hegemony, and energetically set about making the city their own again, offering grateful sacrifices at the Temple mount.

The intense emotion generated by this climactic event is reflected in those sources that describe it, both Christian and Jewish, which are often heavily laced with rhetoric and polemic. Given this literary and emotionally-charged character of the extant writings, it is difficult to know what

Lament for Jerusalem

is the best way to attain to an understanding of this highly significant event in the last great war of Antiquity, which saw the two world empires of Byzantium and Iran at each other's throats. Mme Zahran opts to focus on the key actors in this drama: Kisra Parviz, the proud and ambitious emperor of Iran (ch. 1); Sophronius, the would-be classical scholar and poet called upon to heal Jerusalem of its wounds (ch. 3); Heraclius, the energetic and pious defender and emperor of Byzantium (ch. 5); and two important behind-the-scenes actors, Shahin and Martina, the wives of the two world leaders (ch. 7). In between these portraits she deftly weaves a narrative about key phenomena needed to appreciate better the events themselves: the nature and course of the superpower confrontation in the early seventh century (ch. 2), the feast of the Cross (ch. 4), the Byzantine comeback and ultimate victory in AD 628 (ch. 6), the role of the Arabs in the war between the two empires and their subsequent triumph over both of them in the 630s (ch. 8).

Another obstacle to a proper understanding of these events is that they and the fate of Jerusalem still evoke strong passions and in such a situation the past can all too easily collapse into the present. Yet this is no reason to avoid discussion of such issues and we can join Mme Zahran in hoping for a more peaceful future for Jerusalem.

Robert Hoyland

Author's Note

This brief study on the 614 sack of Jerusalem had to include its background of the last great war of antiquity between the two empires who considered themselves the only civilized powers in a barbarous world, and who paid tributes in gold to keep the hordes of barbarians from their frontiers, but who could not stem riots, revolts and civil wars in their own empires which preceded and coincided with the great war and were one of its causes. The war had lasting historical effect, for the Orient changed hands to the Arabs and struck a fatal blow to rich Roman cities which never recovered, besides decimating the Persian Empire. The seeds of the great war over 13 centuries ago underline events and modern conflicts in the 20th and 21st centuries.

But the event that engendered much sorrow and shook the world was the sack of Jerusalem and the massacre of Mamilla, a tragedy that planted the seeds for the 11th century crusade. The liberation of Jerusalem and its holy places and relics became an ideal planted in the European heritage. The three years' occupation of Jerusalem by Jews in 614 echoes remotely the modern occupation of Jerusalem in the 20th century and the Arab/Israeli conflict therein. The defeat of Persia in the 7th century and the expulsion of

Persians from Mesopotamia were not forgotten by the modern Persians, for they took the opportunity of the American invasion to interfere in the internal affairs of Iraq through their Shia co-religionists with disastrous results.

The great war was led by three men who were figures of a tragedy: Kisra II (Parviz) realized his obsession to restore Persian glory but ended by losing the war and destroying the empire he so glorified. He died an atrocious death of hunger in the vast treasury room full of gold by the hand of his own son.

Shahrbaraz, the conqueror and destroyer of Jerusalem and military governor of the Orient for 14 years, betrayed his country and allied himself to the enemy in exchange for the throne on which he sat for only two months before his murder.

Heraclius, the warrior, the mystic, who toiled for 18 years to regain the lost half of his empire and went to the extreme of bartering his own children to pagans in exchange for their military assistance, and inventing a religious crusade, gained his beloved Orient only to lose it again.

Souvenirs of the war are still alive in Palestine, for to this day the Orthodox Christians celebrate the feast of the cross annually by lighting fires over the hills of Palestine to spread the good tidings of the Holy Cross returned to Jerusalem, but other souvenirs are more gruesome, for the excavations of burnt churches reveal dust and ashes. Heaps of skulls of the massacred monks in 614 can be seen today in the basements of the monasteries of St Theodosius and Saint Saba. In reality the wounds never healed.

Prologue

REPEATED CYCLES?
In 614 AD Oriental (Palestinian) Jews allied themselves with the mighty Persian Empire in the great war against the Romans and joined the Persian army with 20,000 soldiers. Together they occupied and sacked Jerusalem with the Jews slaughtering the Christian inhabitants at Mamilla. They destroyed churches and monasteries and were given a free hand to control Jerusalem. Their objective was to make Jerusalem their exclusive capital and to rebuild the temple but they failed and were driven out of Jerusalem by the victorious Romans.

In 1948 and 1967 the Occidental Jews, like their predecessors 13 centuries before, allied themselves with the mighty British Empire followed by the American Empire which helped them to establish a national home in Palestine. Again they occupied and had a free hand in Jerusalem oppressing its Muslim and Christian inhabitants, erasing Arab landmarks and identity, with calls from various Israeli organizations; friends and guardians of the temple, the Temple Institute, Women for the Temple and others to destroy the Aqsa mosque and the Dome of the Rock, to build the third temple.

THE EMPIRE OF THE RISING SUN*

From a letter Mazdak sent to the Emperor Justinian in which he said the Persians were the emperors of the rising sun while the Romans were the emperors of the setting moon.

CHAPTER I

KISRA II (PARVIZ): AVENGER AND DESTROYER

Parviz: A rancorous and virulent king of kings who killed his father and was, in turn, killed by his own son. A fugitive, a refugee, a humble supplicant who sparked off the great war which dismembered the East Roman Empire and brought about the total extinction of his own Persian Empire.

"Beat the tambours, raise the banners, tell the people Alexandria has fallen" cried Parviz, the King of Kings when the messenger handed him the keys of Alexandria which General Shahrbaraz had sent him. He was speechless with emotion for his ambition had become a reality. He, Parviz, had restored to Persia its past glory, the lands the Achameans had conquered, Syria and Egypt, usurped by Alexander of Macedonia, were Persian again. He sighed as his eyes watered. His grandfather Kisra Anushirwan would be proud of him for what can a man want more than to be the Lord of Jerusalem, the capital of Christianity, and to have in his hands its most important relic, the piece of the Holy Cross and now, after three years, the keys of Alexandria? A man who once was a fugitive is now the master of all the Orient. But a stab of pain suddenly pierced his heart, for what comes after this moment of triumph but the void. He knew only too well how glory passes.

People gathered around the palace and the noise reached his ears but the crowd was thin and not shouting his name. It was different when Jerusalem fell; all Ctesiphon was then on the streets acclaiming him, the Shah in Shah, but probably the people are exhausted after too many cities conquered. This will not be the last – Constantinople is still standing. I want to demolish it and with it the East Roman Empire.

The Chamberlain entered on tiptoes so as not to disturb him. "Do I hear them correctly?" Parviz said, hoping that the Chamberlain would deny what he heard. "Yes, Your Majesty, they were acclaiming Shahrbaraz who conquered Alexandria. His fury rose. It was his war, his conquest.

He chose Shahrbaraz and appointed him to command only on his orders; he planned the strategy and now the glory was going to his slave. But then he remembered he repeated the mistake of his father who chose Bahram Chobin to fight the Turks and who rebelled against his father and chased him from the throne. Would Shahrbaraz do the same?

The memory of his father Hormuzd IV pained him for he was at the root of all his troubles. He suspected him, his own son, of conspiring to dethrone him so that he had to run away to Azerbaijan. How he despised his father, but he was not the only one, the nobles detested him for he was so arrogant that he did not condescend to send to Tiberius the symbols of his succession according to usage between the two empires, and did not respond to Tiberius' demand for peace.[2]

The sun grew dim over the empire of the rising sun. During his father's time it was attacked by Arab tribes of Ma'ad and

Kisra II (Parviz): Avenger and Destroyer

Qahtan[3] and above all the constant threat of the traditional Roman enemies, but the incursion of the Khazars and the Turks threatened the very existence of the Empire. Hormuzd had to find a saviour so he chose Bahram Chobin[4] Marzaban of Rayy, a scion of the noble family (Mehran) a branch of the Arsacids,[5] the Pathian royal family who ruled Iran before the Sassanids. He ordered him to fight the Turks with an army of 12,000 men, against 400,000 Turks.[6] Chobin defeated the Turks, killed their king and sent his head to Hormuzd. He devastated the Turkish capital, looted their treasure and sent 256 camels loaded with booty to Ctesiphon and made the Turks pay 40,000 gold pieces as tribute, ironically the same sum they had extracted from the Persians before.

Hormuzd was furious because he only received a small part of the booty, for Bahram had divided and distributed the treasure to the soldiers to keep their loyalty. The victory made Bahram a hero and a legend.

At this point in his reverie Parviz shook his head and muttered to himself, Shahrbaraz is already a hero and a legend to the crowd who is crying his name beneath the palace windows. I have repeated my father's mistake. I chose a slave and sent him to war. He conquered in my name and now commands the army and rules Syria and Egypt but I will not act foolishly like my father. I bide my time. I will get rid of him in my own quiet way.

My father accused Chobin publicly of keeping most of the Turkish treasure for himself and sent officers to bring back the booty to the royal treasury. The soldiers loyal to Chobin revolted and killed the king's messenger.[7]

Bahram raised the standard of rebellion and prepared for his march to the capital. Insults flew between Hormuzd and

Bahram. The king wrote to Bahram suggesting he should put on women's clothes, symbol of cowardice. Bahram replied by addressing the king as Hormuzd, the daughter of Anushirwan.[8]

The dispute led to my flight to Azerbaijan. The king retaliated by imprisoning my two maternal uncles who then escaped and assembled a rowdy crowd which attacked the palace and blinded the king.[9]

My father died, strangled by my two uncles with my complicity;[10] a painful point which poisoned my life, but then I was enthroned as Kisra II, when the revolt of Bahram was at its height. I tried to entice the rebel with soothing words and gifts, but Bahram replied with an insolent letter calling himself "the friend of the gods, the enemy of tyrants, chief commander of the army" and describing himself as pious, innocent and noble, while I was only the son of Hormuzd. He told me to lay down the diadem and he would appoint me governor of a province, otherwise I would perish like my father. I replied that I was king of kings, master of the nation and I called him my friend.[11] When my effort for conciliation did not work I started to prepare for war with troops I recruited from Azerbaijan, but they were few and not warlike nor loyal but I had no option but to fight the rebels before they reached the capital.

We met at Nahrawan,[12] I with a feeble army without enthusiasm. To add to my troubles my beloved horse weakened and could not carry me so I turned to N'uman, the Lakhmid king who was fighting by my side and asked him to give me his horse.[13] The proud Arab king refused, but this was only his first refusal; much later, when I had regained the throne, he refused to give his daughter in marriage to a

Kisra II (Parviz): Avenger and Destroyer

Sassanid prince, which left me with a bitter hatred against him. I took my time but I killed him and abolished the Lakhmid dynasty and Arab rule from Iraq.

I shudder when I think of the battle of Nahrawan. It is easy to forget the battles I won – but the battle I lost haunts my nights and days. I was crushed and so badly defeated that I lost the throne of my ancestors. Humiliated, I fled my country and the wrath of the rebels and took refuge with the Lakhmids of Hira. But hiding in Hira was no way to regain my throne. The only option left for me was to seek the help of my enemies the Romans. Hira, the Arab capital, provided me with horses and guides to cross the frontier.

Dispossessed of my throne on which Chobin sat as king, I crossed the border with my wife and children and some loyal noblemen. I entered Roman territory as a fugitive in Ciricium and from there to Segiopolis (Rasafa), where Jafna,[14] a Ghassanid prince and commander of Roman troops, took me in charge. He was probably the son of Mundir, the exiled Ghassanid, king and brother of king Nu'man, also exiled in Constantinople.

It was ironic that once again I had to rely on the Arabs I detested, whether allies or enemies, the Arabs of Hira and those of Ghassan.

This was a time when the Emperor Maurice had dissolved the Ghassanid phylarcate, because he distrusted the Arabs and suspected their loyalty. The phylarcate was then split into 15 princes; some of them defected in fury to Persia.

It is probable that Jafna defected but could not adapt to life in Persia so he asked the Romans to come back to their service, which they did. Jafna acted as liaison officer between me and the Emperor Maurice, and carried my letter asking the Emperor for help and protection against the rebel Chobin[15] who usurped my throne.

In my letter to the Emperor Maurice, I spoke of the slave Bahram Chobin and pointed to the danger of people rising against their masters. I appealed to him not only as a chief of state but as a father of a family. I ended my letter by saying, "I, Kisra Parviz, appeal to you as a son who fortune prolonged his misery and I draw your attention to the vicissitudes of fortune"[16] and signed the letter as his son and supplicant.[17] I also promised to give him back some territories including a part of Armenia and Dara. I was then moving from one Roman town to another, where I received hospitality and was dined and wined by the notables.

In Sergiopolis I asked the Nestorian Patriarch to accompany me in Roman territory,[18] but he had the audacity to refuse my request. He claimed he did not wish to meet me because I was not benevolent to his church, but more probably it was because he expected Chobin to keep the throne and he did not want to be with the loser.

My sojourn in the Roman Empire was full of surprises, for I did not expect such a welcome and such hospitality from former enemies. The notables in each town I stayed in, vied with each other to entertain me, but above all they were delicate for they did not show me pity, which they must have felt in their hearts, for the fugitive and refugee that I was, but they overwhelmed me with sympathy. Syria enchanted me, its cities: Antioch, Damascus and Jerusalem, were more than I ever imagined, rich and glittering with monuments, especially the churches full of treasures, bequeathed over the centuries by the faithful. I fell in love with Syrian landscape, terraced hills, lush gardens and orchards of olives, and vines.

Kisra II (Parviz): Avenger and Destroyer

It was admiration mixed with envy, for my historic sense rose from the past: this land belonged once to my remote ancestors, the Achameans who ruled Syria and Egypt before they were conquered by Alexander the Great. I repeated to myself these lands were once Persian and I vowed that I would make them Persian again. Ah but these farfetched dreams of a helpless fugitive without a country or a throne, a supplicant seeking help from his enemies. I was split then, as now, between avenger and destroyer – a part of me grateful to the Romans, the other part buried in the ancient past wanted the lands of Syria and Egypt to be Persian again, a dream which never left me even when I signed a treaty of peace with the Romans which decreed no more war.

Why, why was I evoking these memories of rejection, insults and humiliations? Why did those memories poison my life so that to rise above them I had to prove to myself and to the world that I was the conqueror and restorer of ancient Achamean glory – that I am the lord of the lands, master of the nation. It is the cries of adulation to Shahrbaraz that set me on this painful path of memory. Now the Chamberlain is trying to draw my attention. The crowd is shouting "Parviz the Conqueror", "Majesty, the crowd is shouting Parviz the Restorer of Persian Glory", the Chamberlain said. "Please come to the terrace and show yourself to your people". I went up to the terrace and I was happy, the painful memories vanished like magic.

The Roman Emperor, on receiving the request for support from the traditional enemy assembled the Senators and asked for their advice. The Senators told him to refuse aid and protection to the dispossessed king of kings, for the Persians were without law and without faith.[19]

Lament for Jerusalem

The Imperial Council was of the same opinion and asked the Emperor "Why help an enemy?", but the Emperor did not heed their advice and made the decision alone, for he feared revolutions and championed legitimacy.

Bahram Chobin, sitting on the throne of Persia, followed the news of Parviz and his request for support from the Romans, so he wrote to Maurice offering him many concessions in exchange for remaining neutral in the Persian civil war. Maurice however deemed that an alliance with Parviz was better for Roman interests than that with Bahram Chobin, he also calculated that his assistance would convince Parviz to favour the Christians of Persia,[20] once he was on the throne. In fact his hope extended to the possible conversion of the king himself, for there were rumours that he was secretly converted.[21]

The decision of Maurice had a favourable reception and throughout the empire preparation for a joint military operation against the rebels began. Arabic historians who relied on Persian sources reported that during the negotiations in the capital, Parviz married Miriam, the daughter of Maurice. This fanciful claim is part of an exaggerated legend woven by Persians. Accordingly both Mas'udi and Tabari report the fabulous gifts exchanged between the ex-king and the emperor. Parviz sent a hundred Turkish youths, with golden rings, golden tables inlaid with rubies, and a gold box filled with pearls.[22] Maurice sent back a thousand dinars, 120 female slaves, daughters of kings, and his own daughter in marriage.[23]

Contrary to the legend was the fact that Parviz asked Maurice for money. The Emperor who was accused of avarice sent him a large sum.[24]

Kisra II (Parviz): Avenger and Destroyer

As to the marriage, it is difficult to believe that Maurice, a fanatic Christian, would marry his daughter to a fire worshipping groom.

To this joint campaign, Maurice provided 60,000 soldiers but Mas'udi gives a higher figure of 100,000 soldiers.[25] Parviz provided 40,000 soldiers from Azerbaijan. The joint Roman/Persian army was ready for combat and met Bahram who came to meet them at Canzak[26] where he was badly defeated.

Parviz regained his throne and a peace treaty was concluded by the victors, in which Parviz gave territorial concessions to the Romans. The treaty held for eleven years (from 591 to 602) and the peace was not disturbed except for occasional clashes between Lakhmids and Ghassanids and raids of Arab tribes in the region of Hidjaz which aggrieved Parviz until Maurice wrote to calm him down saying the Arabs acted on their own.[27]

In Ctesiphon Parviz sent gifts to Maurice and gave money and gifts to the Roman soldiers from Persian and Roman Armenia who fought on his side.[28]

As a gesture to Maurice he allowed the Nestorian Christians to build churches and permitted conversions to Christianity. Bahram Chobin, now a fugitive after his defeat, sought refuge with the Turks, where he was welcomed. Parviz suspected him of preparing a coup and knew no rest while he was alive, so he planned his murder by an emissary loaded with precious gifts he sent to Khatun, the wife of the Turkish king. Khatun arranged the murder of Bahram. Her husband, the Turkish king, was furious, for he gave his protection to Bahram, and immediately divorced his wife.[29] According to certain versions, Parviz married her.[30]

Parviz sat on a throne which seemed solid and secure but he was conscious that this state of felicity would not last, for he never forgot the insults from Chobin and that he had to depend on the Arabs of Hira whom he detested, to give him succour and refuge. He could not forget that he, the grandson of Kisra Anushirwan had betrayed his Sassanid blood by humiliating himself and sitting on the throne by the grace of his enemy, so he grieved. His perverse nature craved a reprieve; he must reverse the cruel fate that he brought to the empire. He must retrieve the concessions he had given to Maurice. He must restore to Persian sovereignty all the Achameanid lands lost to Alexander: Syria and Egypt, now Roman territories. His historical consciousness was acute[31] and his ambition for conquest did not give him rest. He wanted to dismember the Roman Empire; to wipe it out of existence. But he had to put the lid on his ambition because of his debt to Maurice.

The eleven years of peace were dull, but he exercised his frustration and cruelty by putting to death his maternal uncles who had helped him in his exile, and murdering his able minister (Bazrajumher) whom he accused of zondical leaning.[32]

He had no more need of the Lakhmids to fight his wars, besides, he feared the rising power of the Arabs, and he was jealous of N'uman, the Lakhmid king, so he called him by a ruse to Ctesiphon and atrociously killed him under the elephants' feet. The act won him hatred and contempt not only from the Arabs of Hira and the tribes of Iraq, but in all the Arabian Peninsula which at the end proved disastrous for Persia.

The murder of Maurice in 602 changed the situation and set the stage for realizing his ambition, although he feigned

Kisra II (Parviz): Avenger and Destroyer

grief and anger at the execution of Maurice. He killed the envoys who brought him the news and put the Persian court in official mourning and vowed revenge on the murderers of his benefactor and promised protection for his son the pretender Theodosius[33] whom he wanted to put on the throne.

Parviz relished the role of avenger for the murder of Maurice and started planning and preparing for war. Gone were the years in which he was living in idle splendour, in a palace so magnificent as never seen before, in which he gathered scientists, magicians and kahins with whom he held regular sessions, especially when a question troubled him. He asked them not only for advice but to foretell and read the future. In case their vision failed he threatened to break their shoulders or throw them under the elephants' feet. A cruel practice Parviz indulged in.[34]

His wives and concubines played an important role in his life, for which he was criticized by the military and the people. His favourite wife was Shirin, who practised Christian rituals and feasts in the palace. She protected her co-religionists, among whom were the exiles from Jerusalem, the Patriarch Zaccariah and others. For her sake Parviz sent to the church of St Sergius in Sergiopolis the gold jewelled cross offered by the Empress Theodora, which was taken by the Persians in one of their incursions.[35] She preached the gospel in the Zoroastrian court and the majii did not dare to protest.

The legend of his other wife, Maria, the daughter of Maurice, is that he saw her in a feast and liked her pretty face. The emperor proposed marriage with his daughter and gave her a sumptuous trousseau with jewels, and robes were bordered with silver. The bride accompanied Parviz in his campaigns against Chobin. The romance goes further, claiming that Parviz informed his father-in-law on the birth of Maria's first son, that he would practise the religion of Christ.[36] According to this tradition, Firdausi claims that Shirin was jealous of Maria because Parviz spent his time with her so she poisoned her.[37] It also claimed that Maria was the mother of Siroé, who killed his father, but these romantic tales are discredited by Byzantine authors.

Parviz was preparing for war, the only way to fulfil his ambition, and observing the state of the Roman Empire. Since the access of Phocas, the usurper, the empire was suffering from riots and revolts and the chaos that ensued. The enemy was crumbling so he planned his aggression slowly and carefully.

He surveyed the situation in his own empire, he could no longer rely on Arab military help after the destitution of Hira. Both the Christian Arabs of Hira, the 'Ibad' who had sympathy with a Christian power, and the pagan tribes of central and northern Arabs, were fierce potential enemies. Other Arab tribes were only interested in raids for plunder. On the whole, Christian and pagan Arabs were hostile, so were the Nestorian native Arameans due to persecution by the Persians. So he turned to the Jewish community. The Jews were well tolerated in Persia and their hatred for the Romans was long dated and well known to Persian kings. Their support for Persia was reciprocal, for in 540 when the Persians captured Antioch they saved the Jewish quarter.[38]

Parviz was aware that six million Jews lived in the Roman Empire, 10% of the population, and only two million lived

Kisra II (Parviz): Avenger and Destroyer

in the Persian Empire but these had greater freedom; they collected taxes and had their own small army.[39]

With Jewish support Parviz could gain an ally behind the Roman lines who would keep the Romans busy, putting off their riots and revolts while the Persian army advanced. The interest of the Jews coincided with that of Parviz: both wished the fall of the Roman Empire.

The Jews of Persia were delighted to participate in the war, but Parviz had to pay for their support and for that they wanted him to give them a free hand in Jerusalem when he conquered Palestine, for they entertained the messianic hope of making Jerusalem their capital and rebuilding the temple.[40] But Parviz had to pay the price for the support of the Jewish communities before he invaded Palestine and to show them signs of his goodwill he allowed them to reopen in 607 the Academy of Pumbedita and two years later, on the invasion of Syria, the Academy of Sura in 609; both of which were closed by his father.

The Jewish aid was important for Parviz, for he had no illusions about his soldiers who were defeated in 610 in the middle of the war by a handful of Arab tribes of Iraq in the battle of Dhuqar. However he knew that the Roman army was dispersed, weakened and demoralized as a result of the civil war and the revolutions. Parviz relied on, and boasted of, Jewish support, for it is claimed that he wrote later in the war to Heraclius "Christ was not able to save himself from the Jews, so how will that same (Christ) save you from my hands?"[41]

The Jews were pressing for the invasion of Palestine but they had to wait ten years after the war started for the Persian army to reach Palestine. Meanwhile the Jews in the Roman

Lament for Jerusalem

Empire were agitating, a revolt broke out in Antioch where they killed the Patriarch.

Finally, a happy Parviz, two years after the murder of Maurice, went to war.

2 Shahid, 6th century, vol. 1, 1994, p. 409
3 Mas'udi, Muruj, vol. 1, 1997, pp. 283-284, Goubert, Byzance, 1951, p. 589
4 Ibn Maskawyah, vol. 1, p. 48
5 Shahid, The Iranian, 1972, p. 312
6 Mas'udi, Muruj, 1997, p. 283
7 Tabari, Tarikh, vol. 2, p. 147
8 Goubert, Byzance, Tome I, 1951, p. 589
9 Ibid
10 Tabari, Tarikh, vol. 2, 2002, p. 147, Ibn Al-Athir, al-Kmal, p. 147, Goubert, p. 127, note 1
11 Goubert, p. 129
12 Ibn Al-Athir, Al-Kamel, p. 473, Ibn Maskawayh, p. 146
13 Mas'udi, Muruj, vol. 1, 1997, p. 285
14 Goubert, 1951, pp. 133, 136
15 Shahid, Irfan, 6th century, 1994, vol. 1, part I, pp. 556-558
16 Goubert, 1951, pp. 35, 36
17 Camb. His. of Iran, vol. 3, p. 57
18 Goubert, p. 136
19 Goubert, 1951, pp 142, 143
20 Goubert, p. 144
21 Camb. Hist. of Iran, p. 574
22 Tabari, Tarikh, vol. 2, p. 148, Mas'udi Muruj, vol. 1, 1997, p. 286
23 Tabiri, Tarikh op. cit. Mas'udi, Al-Tanbih, p. 155
24 Goubert, 1951, p. 149
25 Mas'udi Muruj, 1997, p. 286
26 Shahid, 6th cent., vol. 1, p. 560
27 Ibid
28 Tabari, vol. 2, p. 148
29 Ibn al-Athir, p. 274

Kisra II (Parviz): Avenger and Destroyer

30 Mas'udi, Al-Tanbih, p. 155
31 Shahid, Iranian, 1972, p. 315, note 81
32 Ma'sudi, Muruj, 2003, pp. 280, 286
33 Camb. Hist. of Iran, vol. 3, p. 518
34 Tabari, Tarikh, vol. 2, 2002, pp. 53-54
35 Goubert, 1951, pp. 149, 176, 178
36 Goubert, p. 179, quotes Firdarosi VII, pp. 92, 180
37 Camb. Hist of Iran, vol. 3, p. 579
38 Pagon and Deroche, 1991, p. 22
39 Abrahamson and Katz, the Persian, p. 1
40 Ibid
41 Mozilla Skin, Nehemia, p. 1

CHAPTER II

THE GREAT WAR: PERSIAN SUPREMACY (604 – 628)

The last war between the two empires was a total war different from the wars which stretched over four centuries in which the Persians took Antioch four times and the Romans were in Ctesiphon two times,[42] and different from the second century campaigns of Trajan and the third century campaign of Septimius Severus who created a new province of Mesopotamia and gave it a status of a colony which became a centre for future wars, and the fourth century campaign of Julian the Apostate. These campaigns of the Romans in Persian territory, so called defensive wars against the Persians and Arab tribes,[43] were followed by sporadic wars, fought by their Arab clients, Ghassanids versus Lakhmids along the long frontier where cities were ceded, plundered, ransacked and depopulated but finally recovered. They usually ended by a treaty or a truce until the next round. Christian communities on both sides of the frontiers were often used as emissaries between the two powers and sometimes took refuge in the opposite frontier – Christians from Persia to Roman territories and the persecuted Monophyte Syrian Christians to Persia.

The great war of the 7th century was started by Persia in 604[44] and lasted for 24 years. The first battle took place in

The Great War: Persian Supremacy (604-628)

the Roman province of Mesopotamia, which was taken from the Persians five centuries before. The Roman Empire was in a sorry state under the usurper Phocas and the war coincided with a revolt against him by one of his generals, Narses, Commander of Edessa border frontier. The Roman army had to fight and crush the rebels to regain Edessa instead of repulsing the first Persian incursion in northern Mesopotamia. Parviz (Kisra II), the king of kings, observed the revolts and riots and took note of the religious dissension tearing the Romans apart. The Jacobites, who formed the majority in the Orient, were not loyal to the government, preferring Persian rule to Orthodox persecution. The Jews and Samaritans also opposed the government.

The great war differed from all previous wars in that the Persians' aim was the complete destruction of the Roman Empire, whereas the enfeebled Romans, who were forced into the war, sought a peaceful resolution. Parviz himself conducted the first attack in 605 and captured Dara, a city he had ceded to Maurice in 591, for his support to gain the throne. He then besieged Edessa and started the offensive in Asia Minor.

The Roman forts on the Euphrates: Callinicium, Cerecesium and Zenobia fell in 604/606 followed by part of Roman Armenia, which was conquered in 607. In the early stages of the war Parviz chose General Shahrbaraz, who played the primary role in the war for 22 years and participated in every single battle, his conquests and victories became legends and overshadowed the king of kings.

After the conquest of Mesopotamia, the Persians took time to consolidate the administration in the occupied areas before they proceeded to the conquest of North Syria, with

Lament for Jerusalem

Antioch, the capital of Syria, as their target. Antioch was just recovering from the bloody revolt of the Jews, who had been agitating since the war began, and the Jacobites who were rebelling against religious persecution. The city was also suffering from the bloody struggle between the circus factions: blues and greens, the greens supporting the revolt of the Heraclii and the blues the Emperor Phocas. Conditions were favourable to the Persians so they began their advance in Antioch.

The revolt of the Heraclii in North Africa was started by an Armenian who was given the post of governor by emperor Maurice. He thought that Phocas was not strong enough to fight against the Persians so he sent his nephew Nicetas to Egypt with an army of 18,000 soldiers to stop the rapid Persian advance in the Orient. Nicetas fought Bonosus, the general of Phocas, defeated him and took control of Egypt.[45] After its success in Egypt the rebellion of the Heraclii extended to the capital. The governor sent his son, Heraclius, with an equipped fleet who raised, with the help of the Patriarch and other supporters, the standard of revolt. Phocas was captured and killed and Heraclius ascended the throne in 610. Simultaneous with these grave events, General Shahrbaraz captured Amida and Edessa after a long siege.

There was no relief for the Romans when Heraclius ascended to the throne. Roman towns capitulated without much resistance and the Jews opened the gates of empty towns, for most of the Christian inhabitants had fled. The Jacobites were without enthusiasm and the Jews welcomed the Persians.

The news of the death of Phocas and the accession of Heraclius reached Parviz in 610 while preparations were

The Great War: Persian Supremacy (604-628)

taking place for the attack on Antioch. To Parviz, Heraclius was an anonymous young man he knew nothing about, yet this new emperor had the audacity to ask for peace, and for the evacuation of Persian troops from Roman territory; this upstart needed to be taught a lesson.

In 611, one year after Heraclius took the throne, Shahrbaraz conquered Antioch in a fierce battle in which he defeated Nicetas, who came to the defence of the city with his army from Egypt, and the new emperor Heraclius, who joined him with an army from the capital.

The conquest of Apamea was followed by that of Emessa where a fierce battle was fought. After the battle there was a lull of two years (611-613) during which the Persians reorganized, regrouped and recruited fresh troops.

Parviz conducted the offensive in Anatolia after the lull,[46] and Shahrbaraz conquered Caesaria in Coppodocia.[47] Roman troops were detached to fight the Persian offensive in Anatolia, leaving the East denuded of troops. The next target was Damascus, which Shahrbaraz captured, and took many prisoners. The gates for Palestine were now opened.

From Damascus the Persian army marched to Palestine through the kingdom of Ghassan, with its two regions of Balqa and Huran. Nicetas rushed from Egypt to stop the Persian advance to the Holy Land with an army including the Ghassanids. They had gone to Egypt to fight alongside Nicetas against Bonosus four years before but now they returned to fight in their homeland.

The Persians met a stiff resistance from the Romans and the Ghassanids who were defending their homes and who tried desperately to stop their advance to Jerusalem, for as Christians they considered themselves protectors of the Holy Land.

Lament for Jerusalem

The struggle was in vain – for after a fierce battle they were defeated and the war left Ghassanland in desolation with many killed, including a Ghassanid prince. Nicetas retreated with the Ghassanids and the remnants of his army back to Egypt. The Persians crossed the Jordan and captured Caesaria, the capital of the province of Palestine which they made their headquarters, and from there, with Shahrbaraz in command, they prepared to march to Jerusalem.

After the capture of Jerusalem (next chapter), the religious capital of the Romans, Parviz longed for further possessions, and after three years of preparation he ordered Shahrbaraz to conquer Egypt. Shahrbaraz faced the unfortunate Nicetas, once more defeated him and occupied Egypt, Nubia, and reached Libya.[48] For Nicetas this was the third retreat: Antioch, Ghassanland and now finally from Egypt back to the capital.[49] Shahrbaraz, to show his loyalty, sent the keys of Alexandria to his king[50] who, with the conquest of Egypt, fulfilled his ambition to regain for Persia the lands the Achameans lost to Alexander the Great.

Persian power was at its zenith, their arms were supreme, the Romans were humbled, their empire dismembered and the king of kings was the lord of the lands of the Orient.

The conquest left the lands depopulated and in desolation. Roman cities were destroyed and their trees uprooted.[51] Shahrbaraz was the conqueror of the splendid cities of the Orient, Antioch, Caesaria in Asia Minor, Apanea, Edessa, Emessa and Damascus, Jerusalem and Alexandria. The general who participated in every battle became a hero of legend – a myth. In both empires his name aroused fear and adoration. He was the glorified hero who gave his country military supremacy for 24 years and

The Great War: Persian Supremacy (604-628)

outshone the king of kings and the emperor of Rome, but in all those years he was loyal to his king. He sent him the piece of the Holy Cross from Jerusalem and three years later the key of Alexandria and administered the vast conquered lands in his name.

Nevertheless, he was a ruthless warrior and destroyer who left behind him a trail of ruins and death.[52]

Parviz was jealous. Arab authors who used Persian sources Mas'udi, Tabari and Ibn al-Althir speak of a glorified Shahrbaraz, which aroused the bitter envy of the king, who planned to get rid of him.[53]

Parviz felt he was a second personage in his own kingdom. He must be the first of the Persians, but he faced a hero and the hero mocked him. For it came to his knowledge that Shahrbaraz laughed at him because he, the king of kings, glorified himself with victories which were not his and spent his time drunk amongst concubines and singers.[54]

Parviz had fits of fury on hearing this mockery from a general he chose and appointed – who rose above his station – a knave, a slave, but he could do nothing. Shahrbaraz was far, for he rules Syria and Egypt with an army that was solidly loyal and he still needed him for the conquest of Constantinople which would be the end of the East Roman Empire. It would have been different if the Romans had accepted his offer to put Theodosius, the pretender son of Maurice, on the throne, but as they rejected his protégée, the empire would have to go, and for that he needed Shahrbaraz.

Persia had political and military supremacy which lasted from 604 to 628, 24 years in which the Romans were in an abject state and where the king of kings inflated with glory was the ruler of the lands, the master of the nation, but his

37

ambition gave him no rest. He wanted to prove to the world that he was the grandson of the great Kisra Anushirwan, that he was the restorer of the ancient glory. He must add Constantinople to Damascus, Jerusalem and Alexandria – the splendid cities that were now his – but for that alas! alas! he needed the only general capable of giving him the Roman capital, and yet there was a coldness between them; the general did not pay attention to the king.

The Roman counter-offensive started in 622 and for the first time, the Persians were defeated in Armenia and Azerbaijan. Meanwhile, Parviz retaliated by concluding an alliance with the Avars and agreed with them to lay siege to Constantinople and ordered Shahrbaraz to besiege the capital on the Asian side, while the Avars laid siege on the European side with 80,000 men.[55] But the general did not help the Avars – for his participation was symbolic – he was content to burn villages and churches around Constantinople. Finally the Avars retreated and so did the general, in disgrace with the king.[56]

The moment was now propitious to get rid of the general, for after failing to conquer Constantinople he had no more use for him, but the general was a hero to the Persians and Parviz could not attack him publicly. He had to act in secret, so he sent a letter to a general he trusted who was close to Shahrbaraz with an order for his death. The letter was intercepted by the Romans, to the surprise and delight of Heraclius, for a fissure between his enemies was a gift of fate.

Heraclius sent a message to Shahrbaraz to meet him in secret and showed him the letter. Both conspired to change the letter which now asked the trusted general for the head not only of Shahrbaraz but of 300 military chiefs. Shahrbaraz

The Great War: Persian Supremacy (604-628)

carried the changed letter with the seal of the king of kings and showed it to the chiefs, who, in fury, turned against the king.

The episode of the letter was the beginning of a relationship between Heraclius and Shahrbaraz, who no longer obeyed his king. Parviz, furious that his plan for death failed, recalled him from Chalcedon, which he had conquered, to Persia to stop the Roman advance, but he refused[57] and did not interfere with the counter-offensive of Heraclius who, with 70,000 soldiers, was marching to Ctesiphon.

Parviz sent 12,000 soldiers to Mosul in North Iraq and ordered them to prevent the Romans from crossing the Tigris, but Heraclius crossed the Tigris from an unexpected position and crushed the Persian army at Nineveh. He killed the commander and 6,000 soldiers while the others fled. Nineveh opened the door to Ctesiphon.[58]

Shahrbaraz the conqueror did not interfere for he preferred the defeat of his country, to the king who betrayed him.[59]

The remnants of the Persian army retreated to Ctesiphon, passing through Hira where the Arabs saw the mighty Persian soldiers crestfallen with lowered heads march by. But more misery awaited them, for when Parviz learned of their defeat he threatened the soldiers who fled with severe punishment which made the survivors rise against him.[60]

After Nineveh Parviz returned from Dashara to Ctesiphon and fortified himself there, while Heraclius, in the region of Ctesiphon, captured the Destagard palace, residence of the king of kings, and burned it. Parviz was in a desperate position. He was at a loss so he again wrote to

Lament for Jerusalem

Shahrbaraz to come back to Persia[61] to redress the situation, but the general, suspicious of Parviz, refused.

In Persia, the defeat at Nineveh after 24 years of victory caused dismay and agitation. The country was exhausted, the army was in revolt and Parviz could not stem the tide of anger and frustration, but heedless of the mood of the country he named as successor Marden Shah, the son of his favourite wife, Shirin. The nobles did not accept this nomination, which incensed another son: Siroé (Kawad Shirugh) whom Arabic sources claim to be the son of Maria, daughter of Maurice. Siroé joined a circle of conspirators including the son of Yazdin, the Christian minister of Parviz and two sons of Shahrbaraz, now a declared enemy of the king of kings. The rebels threw Parviz out of the palace and Siroé imprisoned him in the treasury, full of the treasures pillaged from Roman churches, where he was told to eat his gold and silver and thus he died of hunger.[62]

Parviz came to a miserable end, without acknowledging his defeat and without officially putting an end to the war, nor did he show any desire to negotiate with the victorious Heraclius. It was up to his successor Siroé to end the war and make a treaty of peace with Heraclius.

The great war thus ended in 628, with complete exhaustion of both empires, a kind of joint suicide.[63]

---

42 Avi-Yonah, Jews, 1976, p. 257
43 Cameron, 1993, p. 192
44 L. Brehier, Le Monde Byzantine, 146, p. 53 Nicephore, 2009, p. 9
45 Shahid, 6th cent, vol. 1, p. 633, 1994
46 Shahid, 6th cent. 1994, vol. 1, p. 263, note 6

The Great War: Persian Supremacy (604-628)

47 L. Brehier, Le Monde, 1946, p. 354
48 Michael the Syrian, chronique, p. 44
49 Shahid, 6th cent, 1994, p. 651
50 Ibn Al-Athir, 1987, p. 475
51 Ibn Al-Athir, Al Kamel, p. 479
52 Ak-Kurtubi, al Jani, 1999, p.L 6
53 Tabari, Tarikh, vol. 2, p. 152
54 Michael the Syrian, p. 54
55 Ekkkebus, Bob, Heraclius and the Evolution of Byzantine Strategy, Illinois, p. 56
56 Theophanes, p. 446, Tabari, vol. 2, p. 49
57 Ekkebus, Bob, p. 87, 2009, Heraclius in constructing the past, vol. 10, issue I, article II
58 L. Brehier, Le monde, p. 55
59 Mango, 1985, pp. 108, 109, quotes Michael the Syrian
60 Ibn Al-Athir, Al-Kamel, p. 477, Ibn Maskawijh, p. 151
61 Tabari, Tarikh, vol. 2, 2002, pp. 50, 51
62 Mango, Deux Etudes, 1985, pp. 12, 13 Jorga, Histoire de la Byzantine Empire et Civilisation, 2004 (2e édition), p. 80, 2009, p.22
63 Avi-Yonah, Jews, 1976, p. 258

CHAPTER III

THE SACK OF JERUSALEM

Jerusalem, Holy City of God, the pearl in the crown of the Eastern Roman Empire, the religious capital of Christianity, endowed with glittering churches and bejewelled icons, gifts from emperors and wealthy people, its narrow streets teeming with monks and anachronites, with an annual flow of pilgrims around Easter who came to be buried near the holy places, a cosmopolitan city where all the tongues of the empire were spoken, with a population of 80,000 inhabitants on the eve of the conquest.[64] A prosperous city which suffered in 614 the most terrible year in the history of Palestine before the 20th century; a catastrophe the remains of which are still visible in heaps of skulls of massacred monks lying in the basement of monasteries today. The wounds never healed.

Jerusalem, the seat of the Chalcedonien (Orthodox) Patriarch, the official creed of the empire, was rich and splendid, the pride of the Romans and the envy of the Persians.

BEFORE THE SACK
The Holy City was enjoying a period of peace at the end of the 6th century under the Emperor Maurice, who had a

The Sack of Jerusalem

treaty with Kisra II (Parviz) whom he restored to the throne. (The interval of peace protected the city from Pesian/Lakhmid incursions which plundered its treasures.) As it was no longer threatened, its shops were full of merchandise and wealth poured in from the sale of inauthentic holy relics to credulous pilgrims. Life was good. Memories of raids and plunder were beginning to fade. Its inhabitants were heedless of the future as they did not suffer from religious divisions as other imperial cities, for the majority followed the creed of the emperor and dissenters (Monophysites/Jacobites and Jews) were few.

The Emperor Maurice showered favours on the city and built a church on the tomb of the Virgin Mary in the Kedron Valley. The monuments of Jerusalem (Iliya) were more magnificent than had been seen before,[65] especially the Saint Sepulchre and the church of the Ascension on the Mount of Olives.[66] But the beautiful life was brief, for in the beginning of the 7th century (602) Maurice was assassinated by Phocas, one of his army officers who also killed his five sons, only one who claimed to be his son escaped the massacre and went to Parviz for protection. Parviz tried to put him on the throne[67] but the Romans rejected him. The empress was also killed with her three daughters.[68]

Those of the emperor's relatives who survived fled from the wrath of Phocas to Jerusalem, amongst them the Abbess Domiana, and his niece who built the Church of St Sirapion.[69]

The Romans considered Phocas a usurper and opposed his rule, but conspiracies against him were repressed with cruelty. Out of the riots and revolts a rivalry soon emerged between factions, blues and greens, which added to the

Lament for Jerusalem

religious discord that was rife. While Phocas was engrossed in his internal troubles, the Persians started attacking the Roman frontier; attacks which developed into a large-scale war.

Internal agitation increased in his last two years (609-610) with the revolt in Antioch, where the Jacobites assembled against his wishes. This sign of independence was met with a bloodbath orchestrated by his general Bonosus. The Jews of Antioch, aware of the war and sympathetic to the Persians, rose in fury and killed Anastasius, Patriarch of Antioch, and other notable Christians.[70]

Bonosus retaliated by throwing the Jews out of Antioch and championed the blue faction against the green, who sided with another revolt against Phocas, the Heraclii in North Africa. Bonosus left Antioch for Jerusalem where he committed many acts of cruelty, for he was full of godlessness. He turned the blues and greens against each other, for both were full of villany.[71]

Among other acts of torture he killed Isaac, Patriarch of Jerusalem. Bonosus stayed one year in Jerusalem before he was ordered to march with his army to Egypt to put down the revolt of the Heraclii, but he was defeated and returned to Jerusalem where he met an explosion against his cruelty and was driven by the populace out of Jerusalem to the capital where he tried to flee from the revolt but he was caught and killed before the coronation of Heraclius.[72]

Parviz watched the chaos of revolts in the empire of his enemies and noted the agitation of the Jews, who, according to Theophanes and Michael the Syrian, were planning to kill the Christians and destroy the churches on the approach of the Persian army,[73] for this was a golden opportunity, justifying the war on the pretext of revenge for the murder of the emperor Maurice.[74]

The beginning of the war coincided with the revolt of general Narses in Edessa, who, according to Sebeos,[75] to save the town from the Persian attack, sent a boy dressed in royal clothes to Parviz claiming he was the son of Maurice, with the message "Have mercy on him as his father had mercy on you." Parviz retreated and took the boy under his protection. Phocas, instead of fighting the Persians, crushed the revolt of Narses and occupied the town just before the Perians did, but he was faced with another revolt in North Africa, the Heraclii, who, ironically, were also claiming vengeance for their benefactor, the murdered Emperor. The Roman army, which normally would group to face war on the Eastern frontier, was scattered with its different detachments occupied with crushing revolts, while the bulk of the army was on the Western borders fighting the Barbarians. This situation made the march of the Persians through Syria relatively easy, for they met with feeble resistance[76] as they advanced, destroying Roman cities and cutting their trees[77]. Phocas had two wars on his hand, internal and external, but he was finally defeated, dethroned and killed by Heraclius, who replaced him on the throne.

The advent of Heraclius to the throne in 610 brought no relief to the Romans, for they failed to stem the advance of the Persians in Syria.

In Jerusalem there was fear, for the land route to Constantinople was cut after the Persians occupied Caesarea in Cappadocia and occupied Damascus. During the advance in Syria, Jerusalem was probably garrisoned by Nicetas and his troops from Egypt because, when he left Jerusalem in

613, he sent the spear that pierced the side of Christ and the sponge of vinegar given to him on the cross to Constantinople. His retirement from Jerusalem was probably after he was beaten in 613[78] with his allies the Ghassanids, in a defeat that opened the road to Jerusalem. He then retired with his troops and the Ghassanids to Egypt to stop the Persian advance in his own territory. His retreat left Jerusalem without defence.

The triumphant Persians crossed the Jordan where the Jews in the area made their march easy. They first captured Caesaria, the capital of the province, and made it their headquarters, and from there planned the conquest of Jerusalem with their Hebrew allies.

They took the coastal road and turned inland through Diospolis (Lydda) and to the outskirts of Jerusalem where they camped around the walls.

THE SACK OF JERUSALEM

Jerusalem was feverish – in a chaotic state with the flood of refugees who came for protection within its strong walls, villagers from the region and monks from monasteries in the wilderness. Farms, villages and monasteries around the city were abandoned. Troops were absent with no sign of a civil Roman governor which made the Patriarch Zachariah the head of the local government.

Sophronius, a monk from the monastery of Saint Saba saw from the top of the walls the Persians approaching with their friends the Hebrews.[79] The defenders rushed to close the gates of the town. The inhabitants were in despair, there was no way to stop the Persian and Jewish approach, for military assistance from Constantinople was not forthcoming. The handful of Jews in Jerusalem began to agitate when they saw the Jewish columns of 20,000 alongside the Persian army approaching. The Jerusalemites were not surprised, for they were aware of Jewish agitation in other Roman cities, they recalled the Jewish riots in Antioch and they heard rumours of Christian populations fleeing the cities while the Jews opened the gates and welcomed the occupiers – as in Caesaria in Cappadocia and in Acre (Akka).

The upper class in the city, the clergy, professors and philosophers understood the danger of this Jewish/Zoroastrian alliance whose aim was the fall of the Roman Empire,[80] and deplored the fact that the Jews were Roman citizens who forgot their loyalty to the Roman emperor. The Jews were exuberant to hear that the Exilarch (head of the exile) Nehamiah bin Hoshiel[81] was at the head of the Jewish column, and their hopes rose for a role in Palestine, under Persian sovereignty, for they entertained making Jerusalem their capital and had messianic hopes for the restoration of the temple.[82]

The Persian profit from this alliance was even greater than that of the Jews for they had allies opening the gates of Roman cities which led Parviz to reject the Roman emperor's demand for peace with the reply: "Do not deceive yourself with vain hopes. For how can Christ, who was unable to save himself from the Jews, save you from me and my Jews?"[83]

The Jewish zeal spread to Galilee where Benjamin of Tiberius, a wealthy man, recruited an army and joined the invaders in Caesaria. The Jewish contingent however was separate from the Persian army.[84]

Caesaria was captured with no injury to its inhabitants for Parviz ordered the army commander Shahrbaraz to welcome those who submitted and put to the sword those who resisted.[85]

After preparation, the army, with two separate columns, Persian and Jewish, marched on the coastal road and then turned inland to Diospolis and the ascent to Jerusalem.[86] When they first glimpsed Jerusalem, the army was awed by the glittering golden domes, high towers and magnificent mansions and they were afraid of a supernatural intervention[87] that would save the city from their attack.

Shahrbaraz sent a message for the city to submit as had other Palestinian and Syrian towns, otherwise the sword!

Jerusalem was without defence. The army had left with Nicetas in 613, after the fall of Damascus and the defeat in the battle in Ghassanland. It had only the militia of Blues and Greens and the able civilians who would take their stand on the city walls. The city was overcrowded with pilgrims from many nations, Anachronites from the wilderness and refugees from the neighbouring villages. Besieged, it would lack food and water and its strong walls and ramparts could only withstand a very short siege.

The reaction of the city authorities to the message for submission from the Persian commander comes in two different versions, both from primary sources; the account of Sebeos, an Armenian bishop in his history of the emperor Heraclius, suffers from his being not an eye witness, therefore suspect. His account states that the remnants of the Jews in Jerusalem rose against the Christians before the arrival of the Persians. They committed great crimes out of national zeal and did many wrongs to the Christian community.[88] He then states that Jerusalem surrendered, like other cities of the empire and that the Persians appointed commissions to watch over the inhabitants. They also left a small garrison and went back to their headquarters in Ceasaria, however a month later the young heads rioted and killed the Persian garrison and a fight broke out between Christians and Jews. Many Jews jumped up the walls and went for aid to the Persians, who came and camped outside the walls and began the siege of Jerusalem.

The version of the monk, Strategos, an eye witness who was a refugee from the monastery of Saint Saba differs. His account[89] is more reliable for he was in Jerusalem during the event and states categorically that Jerusalem defied the invaders and did not surrender.

The Patriarch Zachariah, who acted as the head of government in the absence of a Roman governor (or even a high official), received the message of the Persian general and was in despair, for how could a city overflowing with refugees and pilgrims from Barbarian Europe defy the enemy, without any hope of military assistance?

The Persians offered a treaty if they would submit, if not, the Patriarch realised only too clearly the destruction that would fall on the beautiful city and the misery of its faithful inhabitants. He wanted to make peace to save the city but he had to consult with the circus factions that Bonosus had transformed into militia. The leaders refused capitulation and did not heed the warning of the Patriarch who pleaded with them to save the Holy City. Beholding their folly the Patriarch was troubled in spirit but he had no option but to defy the Persians.

The city began preparing for the siege and Zachariah called Modestus, a monk from the monastery of Theodosius (Ibadyah) and sent him to Jericho to seek help from a small detachment of the Roman army stationed there. The Persians, furious because they were defied, laid siege to the city. Modestus succeeded in having the handful of troops march to Jerusalem but when they saw the number of the Persian army around the walls they fled.[90]

Both accounts of Sebeos and Strategos agree on the siege and capture of Jerusalem and so does the elegy (lament) of Sophronius which he wrote under the occupation, a few years after the attack.

The inhabitants of Jerusalem standing on the walls saw the flight of the Roman soldiers and began to grieve and wail, while the defenders threw a hail of stones at the army below from the walls and high towers. The Persians used war machines, they put the ramparts and towers into flames but the defenders rapidly repaired the damaged forts and retaliated by sending projectiles. Jerusalem held under fire until the Persians dug under the walls and pierced them with the mengonecos. The men who defended the city fled and hid themselves in caverns, ditches and cisterns while the people fled to churches.

The Persians rushed from the pierced walls brandishing their swords and for three days cut the throats of the multitude of citizens. The Persians were accompanied by the Jewish contingent and joined by the remnants of the Jews in Palestine. For three days they slaughtered most of the people; Sophronius,[91] Theophanes[92] and Eutychius[93] say many people were killed at the hands of the Jews. Strategos gives a detailed description of the sack[94] and reports Persians spared none at all, male or female, young or old, child or baby, priest or monk, virgin or widow. They got hold of everyone who ran in terror, forced them on the ground, broke their teeth if they cried and slaughtered them. They slaughtered infants in front of their parents who wailed and sobbed but were also killed. Jerusalemites had to drain the cup of bitterness with lamentation and terror. If any were caught with weapons they slaughtered them with their own weapons. Those who ran were pierced with arrows. They did not spare those who were quiet and the unresisting. They neither listened to pleas of supplication nor pitied youthful beauty nor had compassion on the old men's age. They destroyed persons of every age; they massacred them like animals, cut them to pieces, and mowed them down like cabbage.

They burned churches and smashed the altars. Sacred crosses were trampled and icons spat upon by the unclean. Their wrath fell upon priests and deacons as they slew them in churches like dumb animals and never blushed before the humility of the clergy.

After three days of carnage the Persians proclaimed to those in hiding to come out and they would reprieve them. Many came out half dead, suffocating and sweltering in the heat, many came out half dead owing to the darkness, hunger and thirst. They assembled those left unslain and asked them to specify their craft, for the Persians were in need of skilled labour, especially architects and masons. They put the professionals and craftsmen aside and dispatched them to exile in Persia. They also exiled the Patriarch Zachariah who had headed the administration[95] of the city. The soldiers of Parviz took the piece of the cross on which Christ was crucified[96] from its hiding place in a garden wall.

Some of the population concealed themselves again in dungeons, ditches and cisterns in darkness, and others fled for protection to the church of the Holy Sepulchre and were massacred there and consumed with fire.

MAMILLA

The remainder of the population which was left alive and un-exiled were sent to the empty water reservoir of Mamilla,[97] built six centuries before by Pontius Pilate to serve the water needs of Jerusalem. The people were herded and confined like sheep for slaughter in the empty pool, with guards surrounding the edges. The pool was overcrowded so they trampled one another. The heat like fire consumed them and many suffocated, others perished by exposure, hunger and thirst and many languished from fear.

The Jews approached the edge of the pool and called to the inmates: "Become Jews and escape death, deny Christ and we will ransom you with our money". The Christians rejected the offer and failed to be persuaded. The Jews were agitated and full of ire by the refusal so they purchased the Christian prisoners from the Persians with silver and slew them like sheep[98]. Blood flew as the Jews killed thousands in a cruel holocaust.

A little later when the Persians understood the extent of the massacre they stopped the Jews from continuing.[99] But some Christians were not at all heroic. Some converted to save their lives, a cleric who converted committed suicide later, which upset the Jews who considered his conversion a victory.[100] A monk of Sinai converted after a vision and a deacon in Acre converted under torture.[101]

Before the massacre of Mamilla, the Persians and Jews were not content with three days' slaughter of the inhabitants, but poured their wrath on churches where, with scorching fires, they set the holy places ablaze. Added to murder and destruction they cried blasphemies against the God who suffered in the same place.

Altars were smashed, crosses trampled under foot, miraculous icons broken, priests and deacons slain at the foot of altars, treasures of gold and silver were looted and sent to the King of Persia. Few churches were left standing. On the Mount of Olives a convent of 400 nuns was shared amongst the soldiers, which led some of the virgins to take their own lives.*

Arabic historians, Mas'udi, Ibn Al-Althir, and Tabari mention how the magnificent monuments of Jerusalem were destroyed by the Persians who exiled the inhabitants. They also mention how the Persians sent the piece of the cross to Ctesiphon.[102]

CHURCHES DESTROYED

The churches of Gethsemane and the Elona on the Mount of Olives were destroyed. The Church of St Stephen (on the ground of the école biblique) located north of the city wall, was destroyed when the Persians tunnelled under the wall, as it stood in the way of siege operation.[103]

Churches in the city were set on fire, mainly the Saint Sepulchre and Saint Sion. The church of Theotokus built by Justinian was partly damaged by the Jews because it was built from reused columns of the temple.[104] Churches around Jerusalem were also destroyed, but the church of the nativity in Bethlehem was spared, because the Persians were stupefied to see the mosaic of the magi adoring in front of Jesus on the eastern porch of the church and did not destroy it.[105] The monasteries around Jerusalem were also destroyed, the monastery of St Euthyme at Khan Al-Ahmar (on the road to Jericho) and that of St Gerasimus at Dir Hajla. In the monastery of St Saba, the chapel of Theotokus was destroyed.

Lament for Jerusalem

Besides churches many administrative buildings were demolished.[106]

The excavation of Hennessy in 1989 found vestiges of the destruction in 614 in thick layers of ash with lots of wood and money from the end of the 6th century / beginning of the 7th, outside the Damascus gate.[107]

Killing the inhabitants and destroying the churches and monuments was accompanied by looting and plundering and the search for hidden treasures. The greatest of treasure and the most holy, the Persians were told by the Jews, was the piece of the Holy Cross in its golden coffin, which was hidden on the approach of the Persian army. The clerics were tortured until they revealed that it was buried in a garden under the cover of green plants.[108] The holy relic was sent to the king in Ctesiphon,[109] who gave it to his Nestorian Christian wife.[110] Michael the Syrian quotes the Patriarch Eutychius in stating that the Persians took only a fragment of the cross.

After three days of slaughter, there were 60,000 corpses[111] lying on the streets. Thomas, a Jerusalemite, with his wife and a group of volunteers began counting and collecting the corpses when the Persians left.

Some were cleft from head to breast, others with fissures from shoulder to belly, some had their entrails gushing out. Some wallowed in the streets mixed up with the soil, others with clay and mud. Those who fled into the Holy of Holies lay cut up like grass. Others were clasping the horns of the altars, others the Holy cross; the slain were heaped upon each other. Others fled to the baptistery and lay covered with wounds at the edge of the font.

The corpses lying in Mamilla and around it were buried in rock caves in the pool.[112] Another cave adjoining it, used as a funerary chapel, had an inscription in Greek "For the redemption and salvation of those whom only God knows their name." The cave, discovered in an archaeological excavation, was demolished by the Israelis.[113]

EXILE

While Thomas and his volunteers were burying the corpses, the Persians were denuding Jerusalem of the remnants of its inhabitants by preparing a column of the elite professionals, artisans and craftsmen for exile to Persia, headed by the Patriarch Zachariah, who was the chief authority in the city. The need for skilled labour was not new in Persia. A number of Syrians were uprooted by Shapur I and Shapur V and were forcibly settled in new cities like Jundi Shapur,[114] Shapur II and Kisra I settled the exiled prisoners in new cities, like the city of Jundi Shapur where Christian refugees moved from one side of the frontier to the other in periods of persecution.[115]

Jerusalem, after death and exile had taken their toll, was left with the old, the sick, the infirm, women and small children.[116]

When the column of broken, wailing exiles looked back at the walls of Jerusalem and beheld the smoke from the burning churches, palaces and their own demolished homes, especially the smoke from the holy sepulchre, they smote their faces, threw ash on their heads, rubbed their faces in dust and tore their hair in grief and longing for their lost paradise and with groans and lamentation moved down to Jericho. The Patriarch Zachariah looked back and said "Farewell Jerusalem, forget not thy servant."

When the exiles crossed the Jordan, sorrow took hold of them. They grieved for the city, refuge to all the faithful given

Lament for Jerusalem

up to fire, and looking back at what was lately their happy seat, moved painfully to captivity and death.

The route to Ctesiphon was long and many did not survive the journey. The rest were humiliated and forced to trample on the cross. In Persia, the king built a new city where they were forcibly settled. The Patriarch Zachariah sent a message of consolation to Jerusalem and informed the inhabitants that the exiles did not perish.[117]

The Patriarch and others were received in the palace by Shirin, the favourite wife of Kisra II, a Nestorian Christian who showered gifts upon them, which aroused the jealousy of the Jews who condemned Zachariah to the king.

After the three days of slaughter and the departure of the exiles, the Persians left Jerusalem under the control of the Jews, who began to demolish and burn what churches remained standing.[118] They were under the delusion that Kisra II would assign Jerusalem as a province to them[119] for they entertained messianic hopes for the restoration of the temple. Their leader, the Exilarch Nehamiah bin Hushiel was made ruler of Jerusalem. He was adorned with royal robes and established a high priesthood and began arrangements for the reconstruction of the temple. The Jews were exuberant and filled with joy in occupied Jerusalem for they felt free from the Christian yoke and they were hoping that Parviz would give them Jerusalem for good and that they would establish a Jewish Commonwealth.[120] Meanwhile, they were in full charge of the city and some Christians became Jews through fear. They appropriated Christian houses; an example is given by the Israeli historian, Mazar, who found a two storey house of a family of Christians in the south corner of Aqsa mosque with a menorah carved in the lintel.[121] For the Christians the restoration of the Judaic cult in Jerusalem was even worse than the conquest of Jerusalem by the Persians.[122]

The exuberance and joy did not last long – for after three years of Jewish control of Jerusalem there was a riot of young Christians who killed Nehamia, a battle took place between Christians and Jews and many more were killed. The Jews jumped from the walls and went for help to the Persians in Caesaria.[123]

The Jews accused Parviz of plotting the murder of Nehamia and their relations began to deteriorate. One reason was probably the displeasure of Parviz when he was informed of the sack of Jerusalem and the massacre of Mamilla. He never wished to go that far. True, the Persian army spread destruction on Roman cities, but Antioch, Damascus and Alexandria did not suffer the scale of horror enacted in Jerusalem, due to the excess of Jewish zeal. A definite change in Persian policy[124] had also other reasons – some attribute it to the failure of the Jews to find treasure under the tomb of Christ, according to a letter from Modestus (who acted in the place of the exiled Patriarch) to the Armenians which said "They who wanted to become the inhabitants of Jerusalem are now expelled because they wanted to ransack the tomb of Christ."[125] Yazadin, Parviz's Christian Minister of Finance, learned of the sacrilege and brought it to the attention of the king, who ordered the confiscation of Jewish possessions.[126]

TYRE

What probably made the Persians change their attitude and their policy towards the Jews was the question of Tyre. Some authors place this before the Persian occupation of Jerusalem (608/609), but a more plausible date is in 617, three years after the occupation of Jerusalem and just before the end of Jewish control.

The freedom of the Jews and their control of Jerusalem incited Jewish enthusiasm and raised their hopes all over the Roman Empire. They began agitating for more power, with the result that a band of Jews from Jerusalem, Tiberius, Damascus and Cyprus, planned to invade and subdue the wealthy and arrogant city of Tyre. In complicity with the 4,000 Jews who lived in Tyre, they planned to massacre the Christian inhabitants on the night of Easter, when they assembled in churches for the midnight mass. Meanwhile the band surrounded Tyre and destroyed churches around it. The Christians learnt of the plot and seized the 4,000 Jews who lived in Tyre as hostages and killed 2,000. To save the rest of the Jews of Tyre, the band withdrew.[127]

The Jewish obsession with the complete control of Jerusalem and their haste to rebuild the temple, for they started a provisional construction on the esplanade, along with the three years of oppression of the inhabitants and the aborted takeover of Tyre, irked and irritated the Persians and caused a complete switch in their policy, and the beginning of their collaboration with the Christians.

JERUSALEM AFTER THE SACK

After the slaughter and Jewish domination, Jerusalem, ruined and depopulated, had a break, for the Persians allowed the reparation of the churches that stood in ruins for three years. The only exception was the church of the Holy Sepulchre which was repaired immediately[128] by Modestus who replaced the exiled Patriarch.

The Sack of Jerusalem

Parviz himself ordered his Christian Minister Yazdin to rebuild Jerusalem and its churches and Yazdin sent a sum of money from his private fortune. The Jews were infuriated by the restoration of the Christian monuments.[129]

Modestus travelled to Ramla, Tiberias, Tyre and Damascus asking for funds to rebuild the churches and with the money he replaced the ruined roofs and restored the looted liturgical materials, but above all he made peace in the city, which allowed again the flow of pilgrims to occupied Jerusalem.

But repairing the churches did not meet the needs of the poor city for food, money and skilled labour, which led Jean d'Aumonier, the Patriarch of Alexandria before the Persians occupied Egypt in 617, to send a thousand gold pieces and a thousand Egyptian artisans to help rebuild the city, for the skilled workers and craftsmen were in exile in Persia.[130] Money from Alexandria was also used to ransom the captured nuns.

As for food, the Patriarch of Alexandria sent wheat, dry vegetables, dry fish and wine for the impoverished city. The generosity of Jean d'Aumonier was especially appreciated, for Alexandria itself was teeming with refugees from the Syrian cities who fled the Persian occupation. The Patriarch was aware of the Persian menace over his city and that Shahrbaraz was preparing for his march on the Via Maris to attack Alexandria.

Some sources indicate that the Persians who favoured the Jacobites expelled the Orthodox clergy from Jerusalem,[131] but the fact was that the Jacobites were a very small minority in a city which remained Orthodox through the Persian and Arab occupations.

In the city people lived in fear of the Bedouin Arab raids, for the occupying Persian army was too busy elsewhere to

Lament for Jerusalem

protect them and the Bedouins profited during the war by increasing their incursions and plunder on both Persian and Roman territories. The evacuation of the Persians in 629 was smooth and complete. No incidents were reported because when the Arabs raided Mu'ta in Transjordan in 629 there was no sign of Persian troops in the Holy Land. The Arabs were repulsed by a handful of Roman troops, already stationed near the Dead Sea and their allies, the Ghassanids, who had returned to their land from Anatolia since their retreat from Egypt in 617.

The enfeebled, mutilated city and the region around it was heavily depopulated and remained so under the Umayyads. There were only eight inhabited sites under Arabs compared with 76 under the Byzantines before 614.[132] The inhabitants remained deadly quiet for 14 years and showed no sign of resistance nor rebellion,[133] for a city full of old, infirm and sick people was too exhausted to revolt.

It is likely that the sack of Jerusalem caused great sorrow in Western Europe, a sorrow carried from one generation to another, for the ideal of saving the holy places of Jerusalem was embedded in the Western heritage and mushroomed in the first crusade of the 11th century, with its objective to free Jerusalem and save the tomb of Christ, as in the 7th century to free Jerusalem and restore the piece of the Holy Cross – both crusades vowed to free Jerusalem and its folk from captivity and death.

While the sack caused anguish and grief in the East Roman Empire and Western Europe, it also set off massive persecution in response to Jewish insolence in 614. In 629 when Jerusalem was liberated, King Dagubert ordered the

The Sack of Jerusalem

Jews of the Frankish empire to accept baptism. His order of conversion told the Jews to accept baptism or emigrate.[134]

The Fifth Council of Paris, meeting of the Merovingian bishops, called on all Jews holding military and civil posts to be baptized with their families.

In Persia, Parviz was horrified at the excess of the Jewish oppression in Jerusalem, but did not go so far as to expel them from Jerusalem before the liberation, as some authors indicate,[135] for the Jews were in Jerusalem in 630 when Heraclius brought back the piece of the cross.

ISRAELI AUTHORS AND MAMILLA

The massacre of the Jerusalem Christians at Mamilla in 614 was a subject both Jews and non-Jews wrote about, but after 1948, and 1967, when the Jews occupied Jerusalem, it became a thorny subject for the Israeli writers. The 20th century genocide of Jews by gentiles stirred memories of the 7th century massacre committed by Jews against the gentiles in Jerusalem.

The situation is discussed in some detail in an article by an Israeli author, Elliot Horowitz.[136] The author quotes Dr Colbi of the Israeli Ministry of Religious Affairs, "The tendency in Israeli historiography, both academic and popular, is to ignore the slaughter of Jerusalem Christians and/or the Jewish role therein, only strengthened after the city came under exclusive Jewish rule as a consequence of the Six Day War."

The article points to the various authors who wrote regarding the massacre in Israeli text books, guide books and journals. Many mention it briefly saying many Christians were killed and churches destroyed, the majority put the blame of the massacre on the Persians and not on the Jews.

Lament for Jerusalem

Others justify the massacre as retaliation and reprisal against Byzantine rule. A few writers deny any Jewish participation in the massacre and say the story was fabricated by Christian writers, but some fully acknowledge the Jewish role in the massacre.

64 Dauphin, C., La Palestine Byzantine, vol. 3, 1998, p. 354
65 Mas'udi, KItab El-Tanbih, Al-Ishrqf, Leiden, 1893, p. 138
66 Schick, R. Christians in Jerusalem, in Patterns of the Past, p. 219
67 Ibn Al-Althir, Al-Kamel, pp. 474, 475
68 Abrahmson and Katz, The Persian, p. 16
69 Schick, R. op. cit.
70 Dagon and Deroche, Juif et Chrétien, dans Orient VII siècle, vol. 2, 1991, p. 20
71 Strategos, Capture of Jerusalem, trad. Conybare, 1910, p. 502
72 Dagon and Deroche, 1991, p. 21, Schick, Christian, p. 15
73 op. cit. p. 20
74 Michael the Syrian, p. 79
75 Sebeos, Histoire d'Heraclius, translated from Armenian by F. Macler, Paris, 1904, ch. 2&, p. 51
76 Michel, le Syrien, chronique, p. 79, Avi-Yonah, Jews, 1976, p. 258
77 Ibn
78 Bendall, Simon, The Byzantine, 2003, p. 316, note 29
79 Sophronius, First Clergy, Cabinet bibliothèque national, Cabinet des titres, M, Latin, 328, 2 XVI
80 Dagon and Deroche, 1991, p. 22
81 Abrahmson and Katz, The Persian, p. 17
82 Cameron, 1993, p. 189, Abrahamson and Katz, The Persian, p. 17
83 Abrahamson and Katz, op. cit, p. 1
84 Avi-Yonah, The Jews, p. 269
85 Dauphin, Claudine, La Palestine, vol. 3, 1998, p. 152
86 Jewish Encyclopaedia under Chosroes II, p. 16
87 Sophronius, La Prise de Jerusalem in 615, Revue de l'Orient chrétien, n° 9, 1897
88 Sebeos, Histoire, trad. Macler, ch. 28, p. 68

89 Strategos, The account of the capture of Jerusalem by the Persians in 614. Trad. Conyfere, English Historical Review, 25, 1910 pp. 502-517
90 Strategos, Capture, 1910, p. 502
91 Abrahmson and Katz, The Persian, pp. 18, 19
92 Theophanes, Chronicle, pp. 300-301
93 Eutyichus, Annales, p. 373
94 Strategos, Capture, 1910, pp. 502, 517
95 Tabari, Tarikh, vol. 2, p. 40
96 Ibn-al-Athir, al Kamel, p. 477
97 The above account of the massacre of Mamilla is taken from Strategos and Sebeos and some modern writers, Israel, Shamir, 614 – The Genocide of Mamilla, 2009, p. 3I, Garitte, pp. 2-6, Schick, R. p. 224
98 Michael the Syrian, Chronique, p. 26
99 Shamir, I. 614, p. 3
100 Dagon and Deroche, p. 24
101 Schick, Robert, Christian, p. 41
102 Mas'udi, Kitab Al Tanbih, wa Ilshraf, ….1893, p. 138, Ibn Al-1lthri, Al-Kamil, Bent 1987, p. 475, Tabari, Tarikh, vol. 2, p. 149
103 Garitte, 1960, pp. 17, 18
104 Schick, R., Christian, p. 223
105 Dauphin, C., 1998, vol. 3, p. 358
106 Dauphin, C., op. cit. p. 854, 356
107 Dauphin, C., op. cit, p. 854
108 Tabari, Tarikh, vol. 2, p. 149
109 Abrahamson and Katz, p. 19
110 Strategies, Capture, p. 504
111 Dauphin, C., 1998, vol. 2, p. 356
112 Schick, R., The Christian, p. 224
113 Shamir, Israel, Persian, p. 2
114 Cam. Hist. of Iran, vol. 3, p. 51
115 Dauphin, C., 1998, vol. 3, p. 356
116 Ibid
117 Les Martyrs, 1925, p. 245
118 Michael the Syrian, Chronique, p. 36
119 Jewish Encyclopaedia under "Chosoes II", Cameron, The Mediterranean, 1993, p. 189
120 Abrahmson and Katz, The Persian, p. 18
121 Schick, R. Christian, p. 225
122 Abrahmson and Katz, p. 28
123 Ibid

Lament for Jerusalem

124 Avi-Yonah, Jews, 1975, pp. 267, 258
125 Dagon and Deroch, p. 27
126 Schick, R. Christian, p. 225
127 The Jewish Encyclopaedia, under Choroes II, p. 12, Abrahamson and Katz, p. 19
128 Schick, R. Christian, pp. 42, 226
129 Dagon and Deroche, p. 26
130 Dauphin, C. 1998, vol. 3, p. 358
131 L. Brehier, p. 57
132 Dauphin, 1998, vol. 3, p. 56
133 Dauphin, op. cit. p. 360
134 Jewish Encyclopaedia, 1826, Abrahamson and Katz, pp. 19, 26
135 Dagon and Deroche, p. 26
136 Horowitz, Elliot, The Vengeance, in Jewish Social Studies, New Series, vol. 14, 1998, pp. 1-39

THE LAMENT OF SOPHRONIUS

FIRST ELEGY[137]

Holy City of God, field of the powerful Saints, great Jerusalem, what laments shall I bring to you. The torrent which runs from my eyes is too feeble for the cruel pain.

Cry for the heavenly city, the centre of the world's desires – subjected to a terrible end. Meanwhile, concealing the flow of my tears I shall cry my lamentation, I shall compose a song on your calamity, on the fate you met.

The perfidious Medes, the deadly assassins attacked your walls, your suburbs. They fought against the emperor of Rome. Children of the blessed Christians come to weep over Jerusalem and wail on its high walls for the enemy marched forward on the Holy Land, destroying the city of God, Jerusalem.

The fiend had risen in fury full of folly and hate brandishing the deadly sword against the divine city… the inhabitants, servants of Christ from all nations, took refuge in the city on the approach of the enemy. Cry for the generations of Christian saints, who, abandoning their cities, their own homes, chose to live in Jerusalem for the love of Christ. Christ himself assumed the yoke of death and accepted the role of the lamb, victim of the hordes who nailed him on the cross so that he would save all the human race, but with signs of sublime victory he rose from the tomb, having triumphed over the power of death.

O blessed Christ, protector, act against Medes who destroyed the city so sweet where young women renounced the law of marriage and lived as in heaven, where all strangers and natives of the city renounced passions for the love of God. Moreover, when they saw the Persians with their friends, the Hebrews, they ran and closed the gates of the city and together they raised their hands so pure towards the heavens.

Cry for the Lord Christ to fight for his own city, the object of the vows of all men.

Resolute, they participated in the struggle; they threw a hailstorm of stones on the Medes and pushed them from the walls. Furious, the Persian barbarians resorted to the war machine under the base of the walls. They lit fires and with mangonecus they pierced the strong ramparts and their troops established themselves in the city. O Christ, train the hands of the Christians against the children of the Persians, who brandishing their swords cut the throats of the multitude, slaughtered the citizens and the pure saints, old men with white hair, women and children.

They pillaged the city of the saints and put the holy places into flames. They pronounced curses against God, the God suffered in past times in the same place.

O Christ give us the power of reprisals to retaliate for the holy places in ruins and let the Persians be consumed with fire.

The Lament of Sophronius

SOPHRONIUS

"The Oriental with the head of a Roman" was how a Greek writer described Sophronius, for he was a monk from Damascus, a model of priestly Orthodoxy and patriotic courage, a theologian and a professor of rhetoric and a poet. He visited the monasteries of Syria and Egypt, settled for a time in Alexandria and became the right hand of the Patriarch of Alexandria, Jean d'Aumonier.[138]

He wrote his first elegy, the poem of his mournful verses and his song of sorrow, a lament, a cry of despair on the destruction of the Holy City and a short second eulogy in Greek, translated to Arabic, six years after the sack of Jerusalem in the monasteries of St Theodosius[139] (Al-Ibadya) and Mar Saba. Both monasteries are still inhabited and have in their basement heaps of skulls of monks murdered in 614. The first elegy is composed of 28 verses from the original of 36 quatrains in classic Greek. On the day the Persians occupied Jersualem in 614, darkness fell, as on the day on which Christ died.

Sophronius shut himself in the monastery of St Theodosius until he was called by the clergy and the people of Jerusalem to the throne of the Patriarch on the death of Modestus in 633/634.[140] He continued the reparation of churches and stood in the face of the Emperor Heraclius, for he was against his unity doctrine. He died in 638 after the Arabs conquered the city. He built a simple oratory in the ruins of the church of St Stephen, destroyed by the Persians, which is today in the Dominican Complex.[141]

Lament for Jerusalem

137 A free translation from the French by the author. St Sophronius, La Prise de Jerusalem par les Perses en 614, Revue de l'Orient chrétien, n° 4, Paris, 1897, Bibliothèque nationale, Cabinet des titres Latin, n° 3282, Ch XVI, folio, 26, 27

138 Marc Swajeer, in St Sophronius, La prise de Jerusalem par les Perses in 614 , Rome de l'Orient Christian, n° 4, 1897

139 Sophronius First Elegy, Cabinet des titres latin, n° 32, 82, Ch. XVI, folio 26, 27

140 Schick, R. Christian, 1995, p. 228

141 Cameron, Averil, 1993, p. 342

CHAPTER IV

THE FEAST OF THE CROSS

The sound of the bells of Jerusalem went up to heaven and for once the ring was joyful and not the funeral toll that was heard in the city for years. Every church bell in Jerusalem and the surrounding villages in the countryside was ringing as hard and loud as it could. The melody was festive after the years of mourning. Jerusalem was celebrating, the Holy Cross was coming home, for the emperor himself was coming all the way from Mabbug with the most important relic of Christendom, after its long captivity in Persia.

The people rejoiced, laughter was heard in the narrow alleys and curiously the depopulated city mustered a crowd – mainly pilgrims who flocked to the city after the war. The crowd pushed to see the procession of the emperor entering Jerusalem, for it was rumoured that he was carrying the golden coffin of the cross as a banner.

The adventurous climbed on top of the walls to see him approach, but the crowd below was jostled and pushed by the Qawas[142] tapping the stone pavement with their silver canes to make way for the procession of Modestus, who replaced the Patriarch Zachariah, who died in exile. The procession was heading to the golden gate to receive the emperor and was led by acolytes with tapering lit candles, followed by a choir trying to chant above the voice of the crowd. The fragrance of incense filled the air and the crowd made way for Modestus, a humble and simple man they loved. They were amazed at his tunic, blazing with colours and his bejewelled crown, brilliant in the pale afternoon sun, for he never wore those ceremonial robes in the years of sorrow. Banners of Christ and the Virgin were floating in the air. The chants of the choir were thanks for the return of the cross and welcome to the emperor. Amidst the cries of jubilation, invectives and curses of abuse were heard from clusters and groups standing in corners of alleys detached from the multitude, shouting and gesturing with their hands, threats and abuse at the crowd, crying "You are welcoming an emperor who sat in luxury in his capital while Jerusalem was sacked, its people slaughtered and exiled; an emperor who left us under occupation for 14 years; and what did he do while we were massacred and our churches burned? Ha! Ha! We will tell you – he had an incestuous shameful marriage with his niece and he showered titles on his sons and daughters and high posts on the rest of his clan. Tell us, what did he do for Jerusalem?" The crowd did not pay attention to the dissenters at first, but some words caught their attention and they fell silent on hearing "You are welcoming an emperor who claims devotion to religion and yet he broke the sacred rules of our Orthodox Church – marrying his niece and bringing her to soil our Holy City, to insult and flaunt our sensitivities. Do you know what he carries in his baggage – a new creed called Ekthesis, which is against our Orthodox belief."

The crowd was shocked in silence, people not in the know were asking each other "What is this Ekthesis?" and were told

The Feast of the Cross

"It recognizes in Christ one energy and one will and is called Monotheism. It is good for the Jacobites and not for us Orthodox".[143] People began arguing and questioning, shaking their heads in disbelief until somebody said "It was made for the emperor by the Orthodox Patriarch of Antioch, who has Jacobite parents, but it was rejected by the Orthodox of Rome and North Africa."[144]

For a moment the jubilant crowd changed manners for they were fanatic Orthodox and forgot the emperor at the gates, until a man who had an air of authority told them "Don't worry your heads, the monk Sophronius is a ferocious enemy of the creed and mind you he will be our Patriarch one day." Meanwhile a notable raised his hands for silence, then said "The Emperor has done this for the unity of the empire – you who have suffered the war know that unity between the Eastern and Western parts of the empire is imperative." This last declaration seemed to appease the crowd and turned their attention to receiving the cross and as their expectation grew they were resentful of the dissenters, who unnecessarily evoked impediments to their one day of joy, and threatened them with blows. At the same instant, people watching on top of the walls signalled to those below the approach of the cavalcade, for they saw from a distance the emperor on his horse in his bejewelled royal tunic and his diadem shining like a halo on his head.

Hearing the news, the dissenters organized themselves in one thick mass and pushed their way to the gate where Modestus, the high officials, the notables and merchants were waiting, and threw a hail of stones at the cavalcade of the emperor[145] before anybody could intervene, shouting "Heraclius cannot enter Jerusalem from the golden gate through which Christ entered. Let him enter as a humble pilgrim without his royal robes, from another gate."

The crowd, shocked and furious, closed around the protesters and assailed them with curses and blows. Surprised by the commotion the emperor heard the injurious cries and saw the stones thrown in his path, dismounted and spoke with his chamberlain who was reluctant to repeat to him word by word the incantation and abuse. Heraclius was stung to the core but without hesitation sent a message to Modestus that he accepts the verdict of the crowd and that he would enter Jerusalem as a pilgrim, through the gate of the column.[146]

When the Patriarch diffused the message the fighting stopped and all turned to the other gate. There was a hush when they saw the emperor dismount and take off his royal tunic and diadem and put on a pilgrim's cloak borrowed from his valet, walk humbly with a lowered head, carrying the case of the true cross through the gate.

The crowd was in a frenzy of joy when he stepped on the threshold and their cries, prayers, sighs and tears reached up to heaven. They acclaimed Heraclius the hero, the saviour, reminiscent of Alexander the Great;[147] even the protesters who stood meekly aside cried with joy instead of abuse when they saw Heraclius come face to face with Modestus to put in his hands the golden coffin of the cross.

Heraclius asked the Patriarch to open the box in front of the crowd. Modestus produced the key kept hidden since 614 and opened the case and found it intact and not tampered with by the Persians.[148] The crowd, old and young, men and women, knelt before the cross in adoration, some cried, some prayed as they embraced each other and shouted thanks to the emperor and called him the "New Constantine, Liberator of the Holy Land, Restorer of the Holy Cross from Babylonian captivity, Restorer of destroyed Jerusalem,[149] Deliverer of Prisoners."[150]

The acclamation, applause and approval brought relief to Heraclius after his humiliation at the gate and as the evening fell the crowd thinned but a huge number followed him to the palace. For Heraclius it was the day of glory, the recompense of 20 years of tireless effort – the culmination of the painful years.

In the palace Heraclius refused to rest, but accompanied Modestus to the terrace, below which the people had assembled. Modestus raised his hands to silence the crowd and said "Rejoice, people of Jerusalem, for the cross has come back home and today will be celebrated as the feast of the cross by generations of the faithful for ever and ever. Amen."[151] Cries of ecstasy followed, "Constantine the Great discovered the true cross. Heraclius has restored it to Jerusalem" and "Constantine the Great built the Christian monuments of Jerusalem and Heraclius will rebuild the monuments destroyed."

Some old men who survived the massacre of 614 observed the scene and shook their heads in disbelief at this mise en scene, this theatre, of the true cross intact in its golden case, for they knew from exiles that returned to Jerusalem that the exiles were forced to trample on the true cross before they reached Ctesiphon,[152] but they kept their silence, allowing the credulous populace to enjoy their belief.

Heraclius was adulated, adored and intoxicated with the joy of the crowd who flocked to the palace to kiss his hand and touch the hem of his garments, but he was exhausted

Lament for Jerusalem

and troubled in spirit and wanted to retire, for tomorrow he would have to deal with the many problems of a martyred ruined city.

On the second day Heraclius appointed Modestus Patriarch of Jerusalem to replace the Patriarch Zachariah who died in exile. He then exempted Palestine from paying taxes. The money was to be used by the Patriarch for rebuilding the churches, but the need was so great it required other resources. The emperor gave money from his own private purse for rebuilding, distributed money and incense to the standing churches and some small sums to the impoverished inhabitants.[153]

On the third day Modestus accompanied the emperor on a tour of the ruins of Jerusalem, the debris of the fallen monuments, the burnt churches, the demolished houses, the ruins of the church of the Elona on the Mount of Olives, Gethsemane and the church of St Stephen outside the north wall. They also visited the monasteries around Jerusalem that were burnt to the ground, St Eathyne and St Gerasimus and the destroyed chapel of Theotox in St Saba. Heraclius was horrified and saddened, for he did know of the damage done to Roman cities by the Persians but not on the scale of the destruction of Jerusalem, and he was troubled in spirit, but he felt some relief as he visited the churches in use, restored by Modestus from the money he collected and the funds provided by Yazdin, the Chaldean Nestorian Minister of Parviz, which restored his spirit and his hopes that Jerusalem would rise again from its ashes.

On the third day he tried to spread his new cult "Monothelitism" in Jerusalem, hoping it would be accepted in the Holy City where he only found few adepts.

His visit to Jerusalem strengthened his belief that the new cult was the only way of uniting the empire. The dissension between the Chalcedonians (Orthodox) and the Jacobites was a favourable element in the hands of the Persians during the war and led to their easy conquest of Roman lands. The unity of the empire was imperative and its realization dear to the heart of the emperor. Modestus tried to propagate the doctrine but he had a formidable antagonist in the monk Sophronius. The dilemma went on after the emperor left Jerusalem. Modestus died in 631 and Heraclius appointed as Patriarch Sergius of Joppa, a devotee of the doctrine. But local opposition in Jerusalem prevented him from reaching the Patriarchate.[154]

On the fourth day Heraclius had to face the thorny problem of the Jews for on his way to Jerusalem he stopped at Tiberias where Jewish leaders accosted him seeking a written document guaranteeing their security. Heraclius gave them a guarantee, for he was generous to the Jews; he had saved them before from a massacre in Edessa. He wanted peace and quiet amongst all his subjects although he was aware of the Jewish role as auxiliaries to the Persians and he knew what they did with the Persians in Jerusalem, especially the burning of the church of the Holy Sepulchre, and of their aborted role in Tyre. Heraclius was horrified to learn the details of the Mamilla massacre and the plans the Jews had to chase the Christians out to make Jerusalem their exclusive capital.[155] In 614 the capital had hardly any communication with Palestine, the land route having been closed after the Persians occupied parts of Anatolia, so his visit to Jerusalem was the first time he heard of these atrocities.

Lament for Jerusalem

The first reaction of the emperor was to expel the Jews from Jerusalem and to prohibit them from living within three miles of the city.[156] This policy was not original; Hadrian was the first emperor to establish such a decree, although it was not strictly applied. Constantine activated the decree on the occasion of dedication of the church of the Holy Sepulchre.

Expelling the Jews from Jerusalem did not satisfy the emperor, for the massacre preyed on his mind, until, two years after his visit to Jerusalem, he decreed forced baptism on the Jews and Samaritans in all the empire, it visaed their families and their slaves, native or foreign and was communicated to the prefect of Constantinople for execution.

However Heraclius tried, the Jerusalemites did not give him any peace, for a week after his arrival a small crowd of protesters gathered beneath the palace, not for acclamation but for insult and abuse shouting "Why did you bring your niece/wife to Jerusalem?", another insolent voice "Why did you tell the Patriarch Sergius to mind his own business when he admonished you?", another sneered "Why did you wait two years to bring back the cross?"[157]

The insolent voices were silenced violently by another crowd which chased them away and called on the emperor saying "These were diehards and fanatics, embittered survivors of the slaughter."

Heraclius, shaken and angry, turned to the Patriarch who was trying to soothe him. "I cannot explain to them my marriage, it is my private business and they are not my judges! As to the cross, they do not realize that I negotiated for two years with nine successive Persian kings who did not know of its whereabouts until I made the agreement with Shahrbaraz – but at a price!"

The Feast of the Cross

The efforts of Modestus to calm him were in vain because he turned to the Patriarch "How can I console Martina who is sobbing her heart out and trying to hide her tears from me? I cannot shield her from their insults. I brought her here because she so wanted to see Jerusalem, thinking that our marriage was forgotten after 14 years – to think that they still taunt and revile us – ah Jerusalem, more vindictive than Constantinople." Modestus was saddened, for he felt the agony of the emperor. "Majesty", he said, "it is the war, the massacres that made these people so bitter – excessive suffering can turn people into fanatic beasts."

But the emperor grieved, the visit to Jerusalem was the epitome of his career, the prize for which he struggled for 20 years, but he no more cared for adulation or abuse – all he wanted was solitude, he felt a compulsion to review his life. Jerusalem imposed it on him for he felt with a sure knowledge that in their hearts those who survived the war blamed him for the sack of the city, for the corpses that filled the streets. He wondered if they knew that he drank the cup of sorrow to the bottom when he bartered his beloved daughter, Augusta Eudokia, to the pagan barbarian, the Turkish Khan in exchange for his military assistance, and that he proposed the marriage of his two sons to the daughters of Shahrbaraz, conqueror and destroyer of Jerusalem, in exchange for the withdrawal of the Persian troops and the return of the cross to Jerusalem – a withdrawal I was unable to enforce by another war. There are things that are better left untold. Did they know that I turned the war into a religious Christian crusade against Jews and Zoroastrians to liberate the Holy City?

Heraclius marched alone on the terrace in the darkness and looked at the dimly lit city and was overwhelmed with emotion – he wanted to absorb Jerusalem into himself, its valleys, towers, churches, the old honeyed stones, its bends on the roads, the melody of its bells, their sounds resounding and echoing in the desert beyond. He cried, Celestial Jerusalem, you are a gift put in my hands but a premonition, a sharp stab of pain pierced his heart – this celestial gift will be taken again from him.

The emperor cried to the wind – why does your light uncover my blindness? Why do you bring back from the deep, the uncouth, carefree youth from Carthage – who never dreamed of the purple or of a celestial city that broke his heart?

The Holy Cross Today

From the 7th to the 20th century the piece of the Holy Cross was broken bit by bit to give to European Kings and princes who visited Jerusalem, a precious gift to take back to their cathedrals. Only two small pieces remain from the original Holy Cross, one in Jerusalem, the other in the Church of the Cross in Rome.[158]

---

142 Guards to clear the way for the Patriarch
143 Iorga, Histoire de la vie Byzantine, 1934, 2004, p. 282
144 Ibid
145 Frolow, A. La déviation de la croisade, Revue de l'histoire des religions, vol. 147, 1955, p. 55
146 Ibid
147 Shahid, I. The Iranian, p. 129
148 Mango, Deux, 1985, p. 113
149 Shahid, The Iranian, p. 304

150 Le Martyr, 1995, p. 46
151 The feast of the cross is still celebrated annually by the Greek Orthodox Church in Palestine and fires are lit over the hills to spread the news
152 Shick, R., Christian, p. 325
153 Schick, R., Christian, p. 325
154 op. cit. p. 228
155 Dagon and Deroche, 1991, p. 25
156 Schick, R. Christian, p. 51
157 Nicephore, 2009, p. 15
158 Father Felix Al-Shabi, http. Kaldaya.article. 5. 2008. pp.1.2

THE EMPIRE OF THE SETTING MOON*

A title given by Mazdak in a letter to the Emperor Justinian.

CHAPTER V

HERACLIUS: THE FIRST CRUSADER

Heraclius, the first crusader, a hero, a legend, a man of darkness and of light, of contrast and controversy, a mystic devoted to religion who flouted the precepts of the Orthodox Church. A highly cultivated man who practised astrology and believed in the prediction of the stars, a warrior who led his troops to victory carrying the cross. Restorer of the oriental half of the Roman Empire, to lose it once again.

The Emperor paced the narrow terrace of the Palace of the Patriarch and shivered in the thin air of a Jerusalem night, muttering in a low voice to himself. He was so tired of the abuse and the praise lavished on him and relished this moment of solitude. He gazed at the stars which predicted his entry to Jerusalem with the cross but had not foretold his humiliation. He felt spent, exhausted after 20 years on the throne – he breathed low, how ironic of the crowd to call me a redeemer, for Christ alone is the Redeemer. Who am I? Just an insignificant speck in the vast universe; an obscure point in this plane of existence. Was it decreed in the design of things that I spend my youth, my best years occupied with a war that I did not start, did not like and did not want? Was I predestined to save the fragile and the crumbling Roman

Lament for Jerusalem

Empire? What makes me different from Parviz, Kisra II, who enjoyed death and destruction? I was informed just before I came to Jerusalem of his atrocious death at the hands of his own son — dying from hunger in the treasure house full of gold, rubies and emeralds which his army looted from our cities and our churches. Alas he could not eat the emeralds and feed on the gold.

Our destinies have been reversed, his from supreme power to a wretched death. Yet he refused to admit defeat and refused to end the war. And I, after 18 years of defeat, arrive at this moment of triumph, carrying the cross to Jerusalem.

What is it in the Jerusalem night that intoxicates my brain, shakes my soul and insists on carrying me back on a journey of the mind? I saw a shade sitting at the palace window of Blackerne, gazing at nothing. Go away! Do not touch me! I raised my hand, thrashing the air and shouted to the wind. Is this young man, 35 years old with features that portray his Armenian origin, myself?[159] Ah yes, I am Armenian, the Emperor Maurice whom I venerated was Armenian, so was my father who they say came from a village near Edessa. My heart swells with pride when I remember him as the Exarch (governor) of North Africa, for we Heraclii have Arsacid royal blood, the ancient Parthian royal family of which a branch ruled Armenia, which was split in two parts — Roman Armenia retained a kind of independence until 387 and Persian Armenia until 427. Christianity came to Armenia in 300 AD, and Hellenic Christian civilization turned it away from Iran, but to us Armenians, memories of monarchy, symbol of independence, remained alive.[160]

My father, the Exarch of North Africa, fomented a revolt against the tyranny of Phocas, and to avenge the murder of his benefactor, the Emperor Maurice. Besides tyranny and vengeance, the real reason was that my father did not believe Phocas capable of standing against the Persians or repulsing them from the conquest of Syria, but at least he could save Egypt.

As Exarch, he had contacts with potential rebels all over the empire and to encourage the revolt he stopped the shipment of corn from Carthage to Rome and from Alexandria to Constantinople[161] and sent his nephew Nicetas to take Egypt from Phocas. When I reached this point in the journey of memory I reverted back to the shade of the young man with the sombre face on which utter despair was printed. I saw him with the mind's eye cover his ears from the clamour outside the palace gates. "Heraclius! Heraclius! You cannot transfer the capital to Carthage!" Other, louder cries "We won't let him go!" The slogans turned to ugly threats. The new Emperor bit his lips. "How can I cope with this situation?" he said to himself. "There is nothing in this capital but ruins, no money in the treasury, no army to speak of. All is corruption – the administration is falling apart. If they won't let me move the capital to Carthage my only escape would be the stars. I will continue my study. I will finish writing the calculation of the date of Easter."[162]

The Chamberlain interrupted the reverie. "Your Majesty, the Patriarch Sergius, the senators and the ministers are waiting in the audience hall and the officials, the merchants and the lawyers are waiting in the inner court." What a surprise! Then I remembered that I had been the emperor for three days. "Let the Patriarch come alone", I said. The Patriarch entered, limping because of his old age, but regal, with a face that indicated his Syrian origin and said in a paternal tone, "Majesty, do you hear the crowd outside the gate? The people have panicked. You just cannot move the capital to your birth place, the merchants fear ruin," he said in a stern voice. I stood up. "Don't say any more, Your Reverence, I shall stay but I did not know that a dissolute rowdy crowd rules the city." "Yes, my son – the Constantinople crowd not only rules the city but the empire and can take an ugly turn."

Sergius allowed himself a large smile and said "I shall tell the crowd the good news, and that tomorrow I will take your vow in St Stephen that you will not transfer the capital."[163]

The Patriarch went out to the crowd which was booing and jeering but when they heard the news they cheered and began to disperse.

When the Patriarch came back I told him "I never dreamed of sitting on this throne of thorn when my father began the revolt against Phocas and sent my cousin Nicetas to Egypt. I was jealous for I felt that my father did not trust me to rule Egypt, but when Nicetas succeeded I had the surprise of my life, for my father had reserved me for the capital and made me the leader of a well equipped fleet, but my mission was only to raise the revolt in the capital and to liquidate Phocas and not the throne. I suggested General Priscus, but he refused, and you persuaded me. I did not want to leave Africa. I am only a stranger here." The Patriarch was stung and said in a dry, chiding tone: "The Emperor cannot be a stranger in his capital."

There was silence between the young man that I was and the Patriarch, and in the silence a button was pushed in my brain, for suddenly they both vanished and I was again a lonely aging Emperor reviewing his life beneath the twinkling stars and the dim lights of Jerusalem, a ghost city.

My thoughts drifted to Blackerne, the palace I have not seen for eight years, since I left the capital for Armenia and the counter offensive. I thought of my father with bitterness – for I blamed him for all my troubles. The old man was obsessed – since the assassination of Maurice he had no aim in life but to topple the murderer, Phocas, and in his blindness did not foresee that the civil war he began was fatal for the empire in the middle of a merciless war. He sneered at the state of the army and was convinced that Phocas was unable to defend the country so he prepared an army and sent it to Egypt, under the command of his nephew, Nicetas. As Exarch in Africa he persuaded the Berber tribes not to attack his territory while Nicetas was fighting in Egypt. He also paid the garrison commanders in Egypt and in Libya where the family had estates.[164]

Nicetas captured Alexandria and subdued lower Egypt in 609 and for a short time had his headquarters in Jerusalem, which he briefly garrisoned.

I resented my father in retrospect, for when I became the ruler of an empire it had lost its rich oriental half. My hidden resentment came to the surface and I neglected my father and with him all Africa. In 609, when Nicetas subdued Egypt, my father thought it was time to raise the revolt in the capital, for agitation against Phocas was growing with a number of potential rebels, and so he equipped a fleet and appointed me as chief of a small contingent, to sail to the capital to get rid of Phocas.

The Persians took the opportunity of our engagement in a civil war in Egypt to advance in Syria as we were unable to

Lament for Jerusalem

re-conquer what we lost. My father did not realize that his revolt tore the Orient, and was one of the causes of the collapse of the empire in the east,[165] and that Nicetas with his 18,000 soldiers was fighting Bonosus, the general of Phocas, instead of checking the advance of the Persians in Syria.

Bonosus, defeated, retreated to Jerusalem where he was chased out by the populace who did not forget his past tyranny and evil, especially killing the Patriarch. Nicetas, to conciliate the Egyptians, decreed a three year remission of taxes and tolerated the Jacobite population by reducing religious persecution.

I only realized the enormity of the damage caused by the civil war when I sat on the throne – but the wheels of fortune that my father set in motion could not be turned back. I was young and full of zeal when I sailed from Carthage. I stopped in Cyprus to collect members of the green circus faction, supporters of the revolt. I even struck coins in Cyprus. I then sailed to Rhodes and other Aegean islands where I recruited more support.

The fleet arrived at a small port south of the capital and when the news spread around we were met by many people who deserted Phocas and flocked to join the revolt. In the capital we had the support of Patriarch Sergius and of General Priscus, the hero of wars against the Western Barbarians and son in law of Phocas, who had suffered under his tyranny. Other long sufferers joined the revolt. Phocas was caught and imprisoned. The angry rebels tore his royal tunic and killed him.[166] Triumphant as head of the revolt I was received by the Patriarch and senators and was offered the throne. I was reluctant because my mission was accomplished and I wanted to go back home to Carthage, but I suggested General Priscus for the throne, who refused it categorically. I was then assailed by the Patriarch, the senate and the populace who persuaded me and proclaimed me emperor. My first act as the head of the empire was to seek peace. I sent ambassadors to Parviz (Kisra II) with gifts and wrote to him that Phocas was dead and that there was no moral reason for him to continue the war to avenge Maurice – justice is done. I explained that we had no design on his territory and I asked him to withdraw his troops from our land. True, I was very inexperienced then, but not so naïve as to believe in the feigned revenge of Parviz – his real intent was to destroy the Roman Empire. Parviz did not answer; he killed my envoys and told anyone who wanted to hear, knowing that in due course his words would be reported to me, "That kingdom (the Roman Empire) belongs to me. I shall put Theodosius, the son of Maurice, on the throne. Heraclius took the throne without my order and he is sending us our own treasures as gifts. I shall not stop until I have him in my hands."[167]

I was left in extreme despair. The universal empire was threatened, by dissolution, and in utter despondency I called the Council of State and told them plainly the empire is under attack from outside (Persians and Western barbarians) and ruined from within.[168] The eight years of tyranny of Phocas and the religious dissension has been of great aid to the Persians. Religious unity is imperative and a formula for unity must be found. The army is demoralized and ill-equipped; it must be reorganized and motivated.

Besides schism, there was famine and plague in the empire and so I decided to move the capital to Carthage[169] to a healthier atmosphere – the consequence of my words was catastrophic. Constantinople rose in arms against me –

senators, ministers and the wretched poverty stricken populace. I had to give in to the menacing crowds who surrounded the palace.

So I stayed in Constantinople and had to deal with the flow of refugees to Africa and Sicily,[170] who fled their occupied cities in the Orient. The local authorities were bombarding me with requests for help, for they did not have the resources to settle the refugees, but the treasury was empty, for the revenue from the taxation of the Orient had stopped. I resorted to striking silver coins from the treasures of the churches[171] to pay the army, and tributes to the Western barbarians to keep the western frontiers quiet. Thrace was under Avars and Slavs.

One year after my accession the Persians conquered Rhodes and Apamea and threatened Antioch the capital of Syria. I ordered my cousin, Nicetas, in Egypt, to rush for its defence with the bulk of his army and our allies, the Ghassanids, and I followed him with a small army from the capital. We fought a fierce bloody battle against General Shahrbaraz outside Antioch, but we were badly defeated and suffered a heavy loss of our soldiers. Nicetas retreated to Egypt and I, crestfallen, to the capital for I had lost my first battle[172] against the Persians and learned my lesson.

To strengthen the defence of Syria, now under attack after the fall of Antioch, I sent the two most able Roman generals. I forced General Philippicus, the son-in-law of the emperor Maurice, who had left the army and retired to a monastery with a garb of a monk and a shaven head, to leave his retirement for active service, and General Priscus, the hero of the wars against the barbarians, son-in-law of Phocas, and one of the first notables in the capital to support the revolt against his father-in-law.

The mission order of the envoys was to improve the defences of Syria, but the mission failed for they found no means to stop the advance of the Persian army into Roman territory.[173] Roman cities were falling one after the other and with their fall criticism rose against me all over the empire. I became a figure of a callous emperor living in luxury amidst courtiers and palace ceremonies, but putting an end to the rituals deeply embedded in the history of the empire would weaken the brilliant façade, which we kept despite wars and disasters, and could put an end to the monarchy itself.

The only solution was to leave the capital, a plan that obsessed me from the beginning, for I could not possibly conduct an offensive from the capital. I kept postponing my departure because I put the problem of the western frontier before liberating the eastern half of the empire, for the western frontier had become crucial after the loss of the orient. Unfortunately I had not given it its due attention for I abandoned Thrace to the barbarians of the Danube. In reality my heart was in the orient but I lost Syria and Palestine.[174] My small intimate circle was mainly Syrian and I wanted to establish a new empire which would rely mainly on the provinces of Asia.[175] I did not relish ruling half an empire surrounded by barbarians of the west.

As to Africa, I am justly blamed, for, contrary to all expectation, I did not pay it much attention, considering it was the base of the revolt that put me on the throne, but I did everything possible for my clan. I put great value on children, for it reinforced the dynasty and gave high positions to my family.

My private life (marrying my niece) caused disapprobation and censure. Condemnation came from all ranks, but I never

Lament for Jerusalem

budged and never reacted as I did when they criticized me for the affairs of state. My private life was not an affair of the empire, it was my own, and I never budged or bent or allowed their censure to affect my actions.

It all started with the death of the empress in 612, which left me desolate, and in my despair I turned to my five year old daughter and changed her name to Eudokia, the name of her mother and gave her the title of "Augusta" – traditionally the title of the empress, and as such, the child participated in the ceremonies of the palace in place of her mother, a deed which shocked the courtiers. I had her portrait struck on coins. She was the first East Roman Empire princess to appear on the coins. Her coinage lasted until 628, after the war ended. As to my boys, one year after their mother's death I crowned my son Constantine as co-emperor, Heraclius as Consul and my other two sons as Caesars.[176] My preoccupation of giving honours and titles to my children, associating my sons with the empire[177] while Roman towns were falling in Syria and Palestine, was much criticized by the people, but I was heedless, for the worst was yet to come – the scandal of my incestuous marriage to my niece, Martina, which shook the establishment and the church. Sergius wrote me a letter of harsh rebuke but I wrote back telling him "You did your duty as a bishop and a friend, but allow me to judge mine." In other words, I told the old man to mind his business. The people of Constantinople, the clergy and my own family condemned my marriage, especially my brother, Theodore.[178] The polemic was rife. I was insulted for flouting the rules of the Orthodox Church which prohibits marriage between uncles and nieces and cousins to the 7th degree. The polemic spread throughout the empire and followed me everywhere and diminished the little popularity that I had. Unfortunately the marriage coincided with the fall of Jerusalem which shook the whole Christian world. At this point of painful memory I trembled on the terrace of the palace of Jerusalem and knocked my head against the balustrade, for the scandal was still alive in Jerusalem after 16 years of war and occupation, and for the last two days I received more insults than I did in the capital so many years ago. Ah Jerusalem, you never forget or forgive – but I only spoke to the wind.

Martina is sick of the abuse, and took to her bed with groans and tears, but I am heedless now as I was then, for I believed, as a handful of my friends claimed, that I inherited the tendency for incest from my ancestors, for this oriental practice was common in Edessa, in Osrhoene, and my father came from a village near Edessa. Much later I added to the scandal by another marriage, that of my daughter Gregoria to my cousin Nicetas.[179]

My friends, my intimate circle, were indignant at my silence and were edging me to react to the injuries and insults that were the legacy of my marriage but I was in another world. I told my friends I have an empire to save, a Jerusalem to liberate, for, ever since the fall of the celestial city eight years ago, my spirit was obsessed with the holy places. My mission was to redeem the cross that the Persians trampled upon and took captive to Babylon. I knew that I had to conduct a holy war and to motivate the troops that will not be fighting for their home lands, to fight for the cross. It will not be a classical war for territorial gain or expansion; it will be a war for the cross – a crusade!

I decided to leave the capital which I put in the hands of my son Constantine, who would rule with the help of the

Lament for Jerusalem

Patriarch. I chose Armenia, not because it was the land of my origin, but it was near the Persian border and easier for operations. It was not possible to conduct the war from Constantinople, where my visits for recruitment of fresh troops around the capital did not yield much. I could not liberate Syria and Egypt which everybody expected because I did not have enough well-trained troops to stand against Shahrbaraz who held Syria and Egypt very tightly. My strategy was therefore contrary to all expectations; to attack the invincible Persia, instead of our occupied territories.

In Armenia I recruited Armenian and Caucasian mountain troops; the Armenian contingent became a decisive factor in victory[180] and I had them extremely well trained but I did not expect them to be enthusiastic or overjoyed to attack Persia, for fighting in foreign lands which are not theirs did not arouse their defensive capacity, but I trained them to fight for a cause, the cross, against Zoroastrians. After years of relentless effort I started the counter-offensive, a new phase in the war, with the strong and well trained contingents of Armenians and Caucasians. I was with my troops during every phase of their long and vigorous training and, mounted on my beloved horse "Dorken" brandishing the sign of the cross, I led them into war. The soldiers compared me to Alexander the Great leading his troops on his horse "Bicephalus", but unlike Alexander I did not seek territorial gain and had no intention of annexing Persia. All I wanted was to regain the oriental half of the Roman Empire and peaceful co-existence with my neighbours.[181]

159 Shahid, I, Iranian, 1972, p. 39
160 Shahid, Iranian, 1972, pp. 310, 399
161 Bendall, The Byzantine Carnage, 2003, p. 389
162 Nicephore, 2009, p. 11
163 Nicephore, 2009, op. cit
164 Bendall, The Byzantine, 2003, pp. 3085, 309
165 Bendall, op. cit., p. 311
166 Bendall, The Byzantine, 2003, p. 309, Mas'udi, Kitab El-Tanbih, Leiden, 18983, p. 154
167 Sebeos, History of Heraclius, ch. 24
168 Nicephore, Histoire, p. 2
169 Nicephore, Histoire, pp. 9, 10
170 Cameron, The Mediterranean, pp. 187, 188
171 Ibid
172 Michael the Syrian, chronique, p. 7
173 Michael the Syrian, p. 154
174 Shahid, Iranian, 1972, p. 319
175 Mango, Deux, 1985, p. 17
176 Zuckerman, La petite, 1995, pp. 14, 15, 17
177 Nicephore, 2009, p. 35
178 Nicephore, 2009, p. 35
179 Mango, 1985, p. 105
180 Shahid, Iranian, 1972, p.309
181 Shahid, Iranian, p. 298, Jorga, 2004, p. 280 called the horse Phelbos

CHAPTER VI

THE GREAT WAR: THE ROMAN COUNTER-OFFENSIVE

In 622, after 12 years on the throne with hardly any military action to his credit besides visiting the provinces for recruitment, Heraclius dealt with the home front by enacting some administrative reforms and reducing corruption. However, after long planning, he changed direction and moved to Armenia which he made his base for confrontation with the Persians and initiated a new strategy for regaining his lost lands. His strategy was unusual for, instead of liberating the occupied territory, he was set on invading Persia itself. He recruited troops from Armenia and the Caucasian mountains and trained them feverishly for a Holy War and infused them with his religious zeal to restore the insignia of the relics of the Holy Cross and issued new coins with him holding his sceptre topped by a cross. His excessive zeal was probably to compensate for his incestuous marriage which compromised his religious authority.[182] In 622, in his first battle in Armenia, he defeated Shahrbaraz.[183]

Parviz was in a dilemma. The unexpected victory of Heraclius in Armenia made the invasion of Persia a possibility, since the bulk of the Persian army was in occupied

The Great War: The Roman Counter-offensive

Syria and Egypt and could not be recalled quickly for the defence of Persia.

In 624, two years after Armenia, Heraclius invaded Azerbaijan and destroyed the royal fire temple, the birthplace of Zoroaster, in retaliation for the destruction of the Holy Sepulchre in Jerusalem. In the temple Parviz was painted like a God with the sun and the moon around him,[184] it also had a machine which could produce thunder and rain. The same year (624), a Caucasian contingent descended from the mountains to North Mesopotamia and captured Amida and Adana.[185]

In 625 Heraclius fought Shahrbaraz in Cilicia[186] and in 626 defeated the Persians near Lake Van. The Persians retaliated by attacking and occupying Chalcedon.[187] In Persia the threat of a Roman offensive made Parviz seek an alliance with the Avars and Slavs with the objective of attacking Constantinople jointly. The Avars had recently broken the peace treaty with Heraclius who had paid them tribute of two thousand gold pieces and gave them as hostages his son and the son of his sister Maria.[188] In 627 both Avars and Persians laid siege to Constantinople, the Avars with 80,000 soldiers on the European side and the Persians on the Asiatic side. The Persians under the command of Shahrbaraz did not help the Avars, for it was a period of coldness between the general and the king; while the Avars did the fighting, the Persians burned some palaces and churches around the capital. It was a symbolic participation.[189]

Despite his recent victories Heraclius was in despair, for besides the siege of the capital, plague and famine were raging in the empire. He did not possess sufficient forces to continue with the invasion of Persia proper or to liberate

Lament for Jerusalem

Syria and Egypt. So in face of the alliance Persia made with the barbarian Avars, he took the unprecedented and humiliating step of seeking help from the Turks,[190] and after much soul searching he sent his ambassadors to the Turkish chief 'Yabgha Khan' asking for 40,000 Turkish knights. He then went to meet the Khan in Georgia with gifts and a golden crown which he put on the Khan's head and showed him the portrait on the gold coins of his daughter the Augusta Eudokia.[191]

The Khan was ravished by the beauty of the girl and wanted to have the original. Heraclius was in agony for he was asked to give his beloved daughter Eudokia, whom he made Augusta when she was only five years old, as an exchange for urgent military assistance. Eudokia became an object for barter.

Heraclius had to choose between his being a father to Eudokia or a father and protector to millions of his subjects, for without support from the Turks the very heart of the empire, the capital, was under the threat of occupation and dissolution and alas, he did not have sufficient forces to continue his invasion of Persia or to liberate Syria. A bleak destiny awaited him and the empire if he did not secure help, but to sacrifice his well beloved daughter to a pagan Khazar Khan, who was in the process of negotiating another marriage with a Chinese princess,[192] was sacrilegious. It was more than a sacrifice – he was selling his daughter and a sense of shame engulfed him. What would the Patriarch say of a Byzantine Christian princess married to a godless Turk? What would Eudokia herself say when he told her to prepare a bridal trousseau for the journey to the Turk, who already had so many wives.

The Great War: The Roman Counter-offensive

For Heraclius the decision was the blackest hour of his life, but the advantages were enormous. He would be making a double alliance with the Turks and Chinese that embraced all Asia, from the sea of China to the Mediterranean, and which would make diplomatic exchange between the empire and China possible. He appeased his conscience by believing that his act was saving the decayed empire from the Avars and the Persians, besides plague and famine.

In Constantinople the news spread like fire and controversy was rife when they learned the ethnic identity of the groom. The marriage was a new political phenomenon for it was the first dynastic union, an outside marriage, never before had a Roman emperor given his daughter to a stranger.[193] (Arabic and Persian sources report that the emperor Maurice gave his daughter to Kisra II [Parviz], but Greek sources do not mention such a marriage.)

The bride, loaded with gifts, her heart broken by the perfidy of her father, took the road to the Orient, while her fiancé was already at the head of the Turkish army, on his way to fight the Persians, keeping his side of the bargain. Parviz, informed of the new alliance, ordered his troops to prepare for the confrontation with the Turks. The Turkish army of the Khan advanced in Armenia, crushing the Persian cavalry sent by Shahrbaraz and badly defeating them,[194] but this progress was stopped by revolt and the murder of the Khan by his own forces.

Heraclius heard of the murder while his daughter was on her way so he ordered her to return.[195] He, by the turn of the wheel of fortune, did not regret the death of his ally and the retreat of the Turkish army for he was on the verge of concluding an alliance with his enemy Shahrbaraz and the presence of the Turkish force was embarrassing.

Shahrbaraz, the conqueror of Syria, Egypt and parts of Asia Minor, the hero adored by Persians, now enters the stage, but on the Roman side; his relations with the king after he retreated from the siege of Constantinople were very cold, for he did not help the Avars on the European side, and they retreated with their 80,000 soldiers and he retreated after them.[196]

Parviz chose this moment to rid himself of Shahrbaraz and sent a letter ordering his murder. As a gift of fate this letter came into the hands of Heraclius, and the emperor acted quickly to use the fissure between Parviz and the general to his advantage. He met with Shahrbaraz in secret and showed him the letter. Together the emperor and the general laid a trap for Parviz. They changed the letter to make it appear that Parviz had ordered the murder not only of Shahrbaraz but of 300 top military chiefs. The general carried the changed letter with the seal of the king of kings and showed it to the chiefs who, in great fury, turned against their king and gave up the hostages they had taken from the Romans and, to show their good faith, gave the son of Shahrbaraz as a hostage.[197]

Heraclius was delighted to win the neutrality of the great general who would no longer obey his king. Parviz tried to recall Shahrbaraz to Persia to stop the advance of Heraclius, but the general refused.[198] Heraclius, unopposed by Shahrbaraz, marched on Ctesiphon with 70,000 soldiers. Parviz again demanded the help of Shaharbarz and his army, which was not forthcoming, so he sent 12,000 soldiers to Mosul in North Iraq and ordered them to prevent the Romans from crossing the Tigris.

The Great War: The Roman Counter-offensive

Heraclius, leading his troops on his horse, holding the sceptre topped by the cross, crossed the Tigris from another side. His soldiers were enthusiastic and passionate, fighting for Christianity and the cross against the pagan fire worshippers. In reality, Heraclius set a pattern for the Roman imperial troops long after the 7th century in which the Romans invoked Christianity when they went to battle, carrying icons and charging with the battle cry, "The Cross has conquered!" The Persians, taken by surprise, were crushed at Nineveh. The Persian Commander was killed with 6,000 of his soldiers while the rest fled. Nineveh opened the door for Ctesiphon.[199]

Shahrbaraz stood aside with the bulk of the Persian army at his command and did not raise a finger to help Parviz. He preferred the defeat of his country to the king who betrayed him.[200]

Heraclius was triumphant: his strategy succeeded. The new army he built and trained with tactics of Guerilla warfare and indoctrinated with religious fervour,[201] erased the past humiliation and defeat. But in victory he only wanted to be alone, to reflect on the vicissitudes of fortune. He dismissed his jubilant staff who were celebrating by drinking and embracing each other with cries of joy.

"Would this victory" he asked himself "erase the agony he went through each time a Roman city fell?" True, he fought with messianic zeal for the cross for Christianity, against pagans, but the only sentiment that enveloped him was the enormity of human suffering that the war brought to both camps. Strange, he felt no elation; only compassion for the broken soldiers fleeing the battle after their commander was killed. But a face tormented him – a soldier stumbled before his horse, stared at him with unseeing eyes, anguish and blood streamed from what was left of his face after it was pierced by the sword. The wheel of fortune has turned; the Persians will now know what the Romans went through.

Tonight, when darkness falls, he will gaze at the stars which will tell him that who wins and who loses does not matter in the order of things when the end of the world is expected. Heraclius, like most of his generation, believed that the end is coming, and he wanted to hasten the spread of the gospel all over the world, but above all he wished for the conversion of the Persians to Christianity[202] before the fall of the night.

At this point he shook himself and came down to earth from his mystic reverie and he recalled that he had a defeated empire to conciliate, and his own empire to rebuild anew, but in his heart of hearts his only wish was for a peaceful co-existence.

The remnants of the Persian army limped back to Ctesiphon through Hira where the Arabs watched the disheartened Persians pass by – so different from the proud soldiers with arrogant sneers on their faces that passed through Hira on the way to the battlefields. The broken soldiers did not know that more misery awaited them, for when Parviz learned of the defeat he threatened them with severe punishment which made the survivors turn bitterly against him.[203]

Parviz, who did not admit defeat, returned from Dashara to Ctesiphon and fortified himself there while Heraclius captured Destagard palace, the residence of the king of kings in the region of Ctesiphon, and burned it to the ground. Parviz was in an unenviable position. He was at a loss, so he

The Great War: The Roman Counter-offensive

swallowed his pride and for the last time he wrote to Shahrbaraz asking him to return with his army to Persia[204] to save his homeland. But the general, suspicious of Parviz, refused.

In Persia the unexpected defeat at Nineveh after 24 years of victory caused dismay and agitation. The country was exhausted, the army in revolt and Parviz was not able to stem the tide of anger and frustration. Heedless of the mood of the country, he was preoccupied with the dynastic question so he named Marden Shah, the son of his favourite wife, Shirin, as his successor. The nobles refused this nomination as did another of Parviz's sons, Siroé (Kawad Shirugh), who Arabic sources claim was the son of Maria, the daughter of Maurice. Siroé, in great fury, joined a secret circle of conspirators against his father, including the son of Yazdin, the Chaldean Christian minister of the king and two sons of Shahrbaraz, who now was a declared enemy of Parviz. The rebels threw Parviz out of the palace and Siroé imprisoned him in the vast cold hall of the treasury and told him to eat his gold and silver, and thus he died of hunger.[205]

Parviz died without acknowledging defeat or officially ending the war. He showed no desire to negotiate peace with Heraclius. Siroé Kawad was proclaimed king while his father was still alive and imprisoned in the treasury.[206] In his victory bulletin to the senate, Heraclius mentions sending part of his army with the Ghassanids to Persia to see how the matter stood between Parviz and Siroé; he calls the Arabs "Those who live within our Christ-loving State."[207]

Heraclius did not attack or sack Ctesiphon as the Persians feared in retaliation for the sack of Jerusalem; he was content to destroy and burn some areas in the region. He probably

Lament for Jerusalem

did not risk attacking the fortified capital for he did not have sufficient forces and the Persian army was still intact.

Heraclius was under no illusion that he conquered Persia. He only defeated its armies in the battlefield. He did not reduce Persia to a vassal state nor did he seek any territorial expansion or aggrandisement at the expense of Persia. He was horrified by the idea of vacancy or a new power[208] and wanted to restore the status quo, for there was no breakdown in the machinery of the Persian government. He was intent on a desire for co-existence between the two powers and wanted to preserve the integrity of the Persian kingdom. He realized that the Persians, although subdued, did not concede supremacy to the Romans.[209]

In fact his victory was very conciliating, for he omitted to assume the title "Persicus" – which in ancient Roman tradition an emperor added to his name after a military victory, like "Germanicus" or "Britannicus" – instead assuming the title "Basileus", which brought him nearer to the Persians with both kingships.[210]

Siroé, who was thought to be a secret Christian, declared the war ended in 628 with complete exhaustion of both armies, a kind of joint suicide,[211] and asked Heraclius for peace, which delighted the emperor who called the young king his son. He asked him for the imprisoned ambassadors whom he sent to Parviz, but was told they were killed when the Romans entered Persian territories.[212] A peace treaty was signed which stipulated the withdrawal of the Persian troops from Syria and Egypt and the return of the piece of the Holy Cross. An order from the new king to Shahrbaraz, who governed both Syria and Egypt and considered them his personal domain, to withdraw, was without response, for the

The Great War: The Roman Counter-offensive

general did not comply. As to the piece of the Holy Cross, they failed to find it. Its hiding place was unknown.

Heraclius continued his policy of conciliation with the kings that succeeded Parviz with whom he had renewed pacts and treaties. However, Shahrbaraz refused again and again to comply with Heraclius' orders for the evacuation of Egypt and Syria.

Heraclius was in a dilemma. His victory was hollow while Roman lands remained under occupation and he could not envisage a new campaign to force Shahrbaraz out of Syria and Egypt because his forces were insufficient and much too exhausted for such an encounter. His only option was negotiation. Siroé died a mere six months into his reign[213] and was followed by his half brother Cabaes (Kawad), who some Arabic sources claim was also the son of Maria, daughter of Maurice.[214] Hormizd followed but died soon. It was curious how those young new Sassanid kings looked up to Heraclius as a Counsellor and Protector and for four years after Parviz died, Heraclius had to deal with nine candidates on the throne. Hormuzd sent him his son with rich gifts, hoping that Heraclius would support him in the dynastic battle for succession. Shahrbaraz would not take orders from any of these kings nor paid them any attention and showed no sign of abandoning Syria and Egypt.

After the death of Hormizd, Heraclius received a letter from Shahrbaraz, excusing himself for the past hostile acts which he executed under orders of his masters. He offered to pay for the reparation of churches he destroyed, but above all he wanted to ally himself to Heraclius. The letter opened the door for negotiations and a meeting was arranged in Arabisos in Anatolia.

Shahrbaraz offered to cede control of Syria and Egypt in exchange for the Persian throne. This barter recalled the precedent of Maurice, helping Parviz to regain his throne, however in the case of Shahrbaraz the question was more difficult, for he was not a Sassanid and had no royal ancestors, and the Persians were very conservative where monarchy is concerned, and attached to the royal dynasty. The bargain was struck – the Persian troops left Syria and Egypt peacefully without any incident. The Muslim Arabs from Hidjaz in their first raid on the Romans at Mu'ta near Karak in Transjordan saw no sign of Persian troops.

Heraclius kept his part of the bargain and to seal the accord he made Nicetas, the son of Shahrbaraz, a Patrice. He also strengthened the alliance by dynastic marriages for his two sons; Constantine married Gregoria, the daughter of Shahrbaraz and the other son, six years old, dumb and deaf Theodosius, was to marry her sister, Nike.[215]

Heraclius helped Shahrbaraz to the throne when the sons of Hormizd rose against him and so, at last, the Conqueror of Jerusalem, the adulated hero, sat on the Persian throne by the grace of his ancient enemy, and the king of Persia was an ally and vassal to that of Rome.

Before he obtained the throne, Shahrbaraz was regent for the child king Ardashir whom he killed in 630.[216] Shahrbaraz sat on the throne of Persia for just 40 days, according to Theophanes; Michel the Syrian gave him two months. On his arrival in Ctesiphon he was accompanied by Christian Jacobites which must have angered the Zoroastrians. His only known act as king was the crucifixion of the son of his enemy Yazdin. He was assassinated by a relative of Parviz, probably because of his politics,[217] and the Jacobite

Christians that accompanied him did not help. Shahrbaraz lived all the war years in the occupied lands and his children were brought up there amongst Christians, which probably led to their adoption of Christianity.

After the murder of Shahrbaraz, Heraclius did not impose his son Nicetas on Persia, probably because he read the mood of the country, for a Christian king would not be accepted or tolerated in Persia.[218] Nicetas fled the country because of the hostile atmosphere and took refuge with the Romans where he became a Commander of the Roman army and fought the Arabs at the battle of Yarmuk in 636, when they conquered Palestine.

The Arabs sent him to Edessa where he wrote to Caliph Omar to give him a command in the Arab army. The Caliph did not grant his request, dissuaded by the daughters of Yazdgard, the last Persian king, who were captured by the Arabs and given in marriage to notables from Quraish. The daughters were avenging the Sassanid kings whom his father Shahrbaraz replaced. The Caliph ordered his crucifixion and with his death, Heraclius' hope of converting Persia to Christianity vanished forever.[219] After Shahrbaraz was killed, Boran, the daughter of Parviz and sister of Siroé, succeeded to the throne, but because of the murder of Shahrbaraz she feared an attack by the Romans, so she sent envoys to Heraclius to ask to prolong the peace, headed by a Nestorian bishop. The emperor received the envoys in Aleppo and gave the bishop a letter to the queen, stating that he would send her military aid if she so requested. On the return of the envoys, the bishop had trouble with his fellow Nestorians because he celebrated the Greek Orthodox liturgy with the emperor.

Lament for Jerusalem

Heraclius, obsessed with religious unity, came to the rescue of the bishop and sent back a letter saying he was in accord with the Nestorians, because he hoped for a union with the church of Persia.

Boran was succeeded by Hormizd who, like his predecessors, sent his son to be protected by the emperor and kept Persia under the wing of Heraclius.[220]

Heraclius was soon enveloped with lassitude from Persian intrigues and dynastic quarrels, for he was preoccupied with the Arab invasion which started with the incursion of Mu'ta in 629, followed by the conquest of Palestine, Syria and Egypt. Once again he lost the Orient he loved. According to Michael the Syrian, he retreated after the battle of Yarmuk on the road of shame, his glory and good fortune had left him. Passing amidst the stupefied population of Syria, he had no consolation, for the Patriarch Sergius was no longer there to console him. He left Jerusalem in the hands of Sophronius. At the end of the province he turned with uncontrolled emotion and said, "Adieu, Syria" for the last time.

In the capital he concentrated his attention on safeguarding the remaining Western half of the empire from Barbarian attacks. He kept working on the "Ekthesis", his obsession with the unity between east and west, although the East he wanted to unite with was lost forever.

He died in 641 from dropsy, a disease in which watery fluid collects in some parts of the body, and in his testament he asked his children from the first marriage to take care of his beloved Martina.

Heraclius had no hopes of ever regaining the Orient, or of building a new empire, but he could not forget Jerusalem

The Great War: The Roman Counter-offensive

nor forgive himself for losing her twice, the loss irked him by day and haunted his dreams. He pleaded with the celestial city to give him peace but it was dumb to his pleas: to console himself he cried "O, Jerusalem, why do I grieve for you when you are not eternal and will vanish when the world ends!"

182 Forlow, La Deviation, 1955, p. 53
183 Ekkebus, Heraclius, p. 82
184 Nicephore, 2009; p. 18
185 Jorga, Histoire, 2004, p. 27, quotes Sabers, pp. 80-89
186 Zucherman, La petite, 1995, p. 117
187 L. Brehir, Le Monde Byzantin, 1946, p. 55
188 Nicephore, p. 27
189 Mango, 1995, pp. 106, 107
190 Nicephore, 2009, p. 17
191 Jorga, p. 70, L. Brehier, Le Monde, p. 56
192 Zuckermann, 1995, p. 117
193 Zuckerman, p. 122
194 Michael the Syrian, Chronique, p. 154
195 Zuckerman, pp. 120, 121
196 Ekkebus Bob, Heraclius, p.56, Theophore, p. 146, Tabari, vol. 2, p. 49
197 Mango, p 107
198 Ekkebus, 2009, p. 87
199 L. Brehier, Le Monde, p. 55, Ibn Al-Althir, p. 477
200 Mango, 1955, pp. 108, 109, quotes Michael the Syrian
201 L. Brehier, p. 55, Ekkebus, Bob, p. 81
202 Mango, Deux, p. 118
203 Ibn Al-Althir, Al-Kamel, pà. 477, Ibn Maskaroyah, p. 151
204 Tabari, Tarikh, vol. 2, 2002, pp. 50, 51
205 Mango, 1985, pp. 12, 13, Jorga History, 2004, p. 801, Nicephore, 2009, p. 22
206 Shahid, 6th cent, vol. 1, 1995, p. 642
207 Ibid
208 Ubierina, Pablo, 200, p. 5

Lament for Jerusalem

209 Shahid, Iranian, 1972, pp. 297, 306
210 Shahid, Iranian, 1972, p. 308
211 Necephore, 2009, p. 23
212 Avi-Yonah, Jews, p. 258
213 Mango, 1995, p. 19
214 Shahid, Iranian, 1972
215 Zucherman, La Petite, p. 118, 119
216 Nicephore, 2009, p. 109
217 Mango, 1985, p. 115
218 Ibid
219 Mango, 1985, pp. 116, 117
220 Mango, 1985, pp. 115, 116

CHAPTER VII

TWO SIRENS: SHIRIN AND MARTINA

Shirin and Martina did not have wings like sirens of ancient lore whose songs charmed sailors and led them to death, but they were women who attract and are dangerous to men.

Kisra II (Parviz) and Heraclius, antagonists to death, shared the same obsession; they were besotted by their women who brought them to destruction.

Parviz, when chased from the palace and imprisoned in the vast treasury hall, had only thoughts for the safety of Shirin, for he was ignorant of her fate. "Shirin" he cried, his voice echoing through the empty hall, "what have they done to you?" In his grief he smote his cheeks, a gesture that only women do in a funerary procession. "Did that dog, Siroè murder you in cold blood avenging his mother Maria?"[221] Malicious court rumours claimed Shirin poisoned Maria out of jealousy because Parviz had paid her too much attention. It is true, he thought, Shirin is very possessive, she made me shun my other wives and concubines.

Parviz shivered in the cold room, his bones were aching, the light from the two windows in the ceiling was fading. There was not a divan or carpet in the room to sit upon so he pulled a block of wood from a cabinet and sat upon the floor.

Lament for Jerusalem

He was hungry but surely the slave would soon bring him dinner, for he did not take seriously the parting words of Siroè: "Now you can eat all the gold and silver you horded, unless you prefer to eat emeralds"; that was a bad joke from his traitor son. Ah, he heard footsteps outside the hall – "Guard! Guard!" he shouted "Bring a jug of wine with my dinner." He waited until the footsteps sounded near and then heard the sneering voice of his former valet, "Majesty, my orders are that tonight your dinner is rubies with gold, or silver if you prefer? Your breakfast will be lapis lazuli with turquoise", he said with a harsh laugh. Parviz called out "I am the Shah in Shah, your Master, the grandson of Kisra Anushirwan, how dare you speak to me in that sneering voice? Can you tell me what they did to Shirin?" The footsteps of the voice vanished. Parviz got up from the floor and looked around at the cabinets full of jewels – those on the right side were new cabinets full of the plunder and loot from the churches of Jerusalem – icons of the mother of God studded with jewels, halos of gold plucked from the heads of angels – this is what Shahrbaraz sent me, but how much did he and his soldiers appropriate for themselves? And the thought of the slaughter and massacre of Jerusalem pinched his heart. It is the only time in all my years with Shirin that I heard her wail for the Christians of Jerusalem – she never reproached me or asked me about the war, not even after Jerusalem, but I knew she talked with Yazadin, my Minister, who is a Chaldean Nestorian Christian like herself. "Shirin," I said to her, "I am also saddened by what my soldiers and the Jews did in Jerusalem. I never thought they would go that far." "Majesty," she said in a broken voice, "you are the Lord and the Master, it is not for me to question your deeds and decisions."

Two Sirens: Shirin and Martina

It was cold and damp so I went to the cabinet where they put the looted ceremonial robes of the priests of Jerusalem. I began to throw them out on the floor, beautiful silks that shone with their silver threads. I put two of the thickest robes around my shoulders and made a bed of the rest and lay down. I must have dozed for I heard heavy thuds on the floor and a wail like that of an animal and words in Arabic which I did not understand that I must be dreaming: that must be N'uman the king of Hira being trampled under the feet of my elephants. I put my hands to my ears. He must be shouting maledictions "Stop, stop your coarse invectives – stop invoking your Christian God. You cursed me when your soul was leaving your body and your gods listened, but my gods alas have deaf ears since Heraclius burnt their temple of the sun in Azerbaijan."

I got up from the floor and started pacing around the room, but then laid down and again dreams assailed me, but now instead of Arabic I hear maledictions in elegant Persian. That must be Bazrajumher whose words of wisdom enchanted the public and whom I sent to my stable of elephants on a false accusation. Ah Ahura Mazda – I never knew that our language had so many curses. He knows now that his curses are realized, my fate is worse than his. The shades of more victims appear. Where do I run away from all this screaming crowd of magicians, seers and astrologists, merchants and officials who I sent to the stables – those who gave me rosy false predictions, because they did not dare to tell me the deep bottomless abyss they saw in my future. Silence for a while, but now I hear choking gurgles. It must be my father when my uncles strangled him with my consent. I cannot bear it anymore. All my victims have

Lament for Jerusalem

leagued against me. I wonder if they knew how I was victimized. I was kicked out of my country. I lost my throne. I was a desolate refugee. I humbled myself to my enemies.

My dreams vanished, "Shirin, Shirin" I cried, "come to me; drive them away; let me lie on your shoulder." Alas, my voice was muffled by the void. I stamped my feet and looked again on the plunder from Jerusalem: the icons studded with rubies, the virgin in a frame of precious stones, the silver and gold plate from the palaces of the rich merchants – but this was only a small part of the treasures. Shahrbaraz and his soldiers appropriated the main part for themselves. To think I owned all this and now I am hungry and want my breakfast. Siroé cannot be serious but I heard again his deadly mocking insults before the guards held me tight. "You only listened to that whore of yours. You were blind to the region of Ctesiphon destroyed and burnt, the army was on the brink of revolt, the people were impoverished and exhausted. You refused to negotiate with Heraclius, your only care was for the Chaldean harlot, for her you ignored the Sassanid dynastic rules, you broke the law, you bypassed me, your eldest son, for the son of your favourite, whose intelligence is that of a donkey. The nobles and the magi were affronted, so were the people, to have as king the son of a non-Persian Chaldean Christian. Did her charms make you forget that I was the heir to the throne? She bewitched you, you made her queen over the other wives – she preached the gospel in the palace under the noses of the magi. Did you ever notice the hate on their faces when she passed? You could have redressed Persia's defeat and agitation instead of naming your successor."

"Stop" I cried, I wanted to strangle him, for he never dared to insult Shirin before, but two guards held me back. He

Two Sirens: Shirin and Martina

mocked, jeered and laughed rudely in my face. "You can feed on the treasures you horded" and left the hall. I was speechless. My only thought was why I did not imprison and kill him when they reported to me that he was a secret Christian.

I laid on the priestly robes and dozed, hunger and thirst were beginning to act on my brain and in this state of half sleep I relived the last scene with Shirin. I remembered how I returned to Ctesiphon and closeted myself in an upper room in the palace after they informed me of the shameful defeat at Nineveh. I was angry with the military chiefs and called them to strengthen the fortifications in the capital, for the enemy aimed at destroying Ctesiphon in retaliation for our destruction of Jerusalem. I grieved for the glory that had passed and sought my only consolation with Shirin.

Shirin had spent her days with her maids in the bath in anticipation of my visit. She was massaged and anointed with the most precious perfumes of India and Arabia. Her long lustrous black hair was washed with extracts of musk and roses – she waited, for I had called all the Chaldean priests to predict my fortune, but what future have I left after defeat? The priests did not tell me the darkness they saw in my horoscope, but for once I understood and dismissed them without threats. I went to Shirin, her apartment was the brightest and richest in the palace, she was waiting in her transparent muslin robe, like a willow tree bending in the wind. She rushed towards me, kissed my hands, my feet, the hem of my tunic and enveloped me with her long hair. I was intoxicated with her perfume of rose and amber and the incense of Arabia that filled the room. Her eyes were full of tears as she whispered "my love, my dear, my lord, my only one." I raised her up and took her in my

Lament for Jerusalem

arms. "My gazelle of the Arabian desert." "I grieve for you," she said, "but Nineveh is not the end of the world". "Hush, hush, my love – do not talk of defeat." She stroked my cheek as she handed me a jewelled cup full of gold nectar which she alone knew how to make, for she was handed the recipe by an old priest in a monastery near Hira, and she refused to give the secret recipe to the wine master or the cook of the palace. She stretched herself at my feet and I gazed at the harmony of her features, her chiselled nose, her dark eyes, which drove me to madness, her pale white skin. I contemplated her beauty in silence and my nerves relaxed. "Come, come my love, why do I see tears in your eyes? I will have the moon descend from heaven if you so wish." "Will you?" she said in a faint voice. "I promise. Now tell me why do you cry?" She entwined herself in my arms and said "My informers within and outside of the palace tell me the army is resentful, the people are angry. Intrigues and conspiracies are all around us in the dark." She choked, breathless and stopped. "Go on – tell me the worst" I insisted. She hesitated, "They say that when Siroé gets the throne he will humiliate and murder me because I am your favourite." "Stop, Shirin." I was very angry "Who says that Siroé will get the throne. I am not dead yet and I haven't named a successor!" "My Lord," she said, "you know they all hate me because I am not Persian and they despise me as a Nestorian Chaldean." "They envy you, they are only jealous of your beauty my love and you are not a foreigner, the Chaldeans are my subjects like the Persians." "My Lord, I am helpless without your protection." "Shirin, you are speaking of my death. Siroé will not succeed me. Tell me, is our son Mardan Shah old enough to mount the throne?" "He has come of

Two Sirens: Shirin and Martina

age my Lord." "Your son will rule after me. I shall name him as the future Shah in Shah. You see, alive and dead you are under my protection. Tomorrow I will announce Mardan Shah as the Crown Prince. Come closer and fill my cup with your nectar." I fell asleep in her arms and like sailors on the wide seas I listened to the music of the siren and like the sailor I fell to my destruction.

The next day, cloudy with a drizzle of rain, Parviz called the council and announced his successor. When the news spread the nobles were furious, the conservative populace resented the king flouting dynastic rules, and agitation covered the land. His enemies enjoyed saying he preferred Shirin to his country. Parviz ignored the gossip and took refuge in the arms of Shirin.

Siroé, the son he bypassed, joined a rebel circle which stormed the palace, pulled Parviz from Shirin's arms, who was trembling and crying in her night dress. The guards of the palace joined the conspirators and followed his son who locked him in the treasury and told him "Now you can eat your treasures until you die."

MARTINA

The Empress Eudokia had a grandiose funeral, four years after her husband came to the throne. She died of epilepsy after suffering from violent seizures. The emperor grieved but did not stay celibate for long, for in the middle of the great war he contracted an incestuous marriage with his niece Martina, daughter of his sister Maria – a sacrilegious marriage which shocked the whole empire. The Patriarch of Constantinople admonished him for breaking the rules of the Orthodox Church but was told to mind his own business. All society

Lament for Jerusalem

was repulsed by the marriage, including his own imperial family.

There was no justification or explanation of such an act, except that some attributed it to an oriental practice, inherited by the emperor from his ancestors who lived near Edessa. The objection to the marriage was accentuated because it was timed with the fall of Roman cities, above all that of Jerusalem. Condemnation was universal and the popularity of the emperor was reduced to the lowest level, his authority as the head of the Orthodox Church was in question, whilst the empire was crumbling near to dissolution. His young brother, Theodore, to whom Heraclius had given a high post,[222] rose against him and was severely punished.

The whole world rose against him, but Heraclius, a cultivated man devoted to religion, was heedless of public opinion because he was besotted by Martina and under her magic spell and feminine wiles. He heard nothing but her hushed childish voice and was drowned in her large and translucent green eyes. His world was her silken languid body and her breath was of carnation and musk. He adored her long swanlike neck and her pouting lips. To him she was love and joy incarnate – his recompense for the thorny life he led. Thousands of Roman soldiers killed, the flood of refugees from Roman towns: she was his consolation against war and death. The public was scandalized that he spent his time in his shameful marriage, instead of saving the Orient. His children from his first wife resented and hated their cousin Martina, the atmosphere in the palace was poisonous.

No-one in the palace understood how Martina ensnared him. Her own mother, Maria, was not aware of how her daughter seduced her uncle. The adolescent had blossomed into a voluptuous beauty and ever since the empress died she followed Heraclius with her adoring green eyes and wore revealing robes in his presence. He was flattered, he indulged his niece, called her his little lamb, and caressed her blond hair.

Eudokia, Heraclius' daughter, was of the same age as Martina and saw, with her feminine instinct, Martina's seductions, but when she told her brothers they dismissed this as jealousy, for Martina was very beautiful.

The marriage fell as a thunderbolt over Constantinople, the news was unbelievable. There was agitation and conspiracy, Heraclius was about to lose his throne because of the siren Martina.

His own family, including his illegitimate sons, rose against him. Reports reached him that his own son and his nephew were conspiring with some of their friends to dethrone him. For punishment he ordered their heads shaved and their noses cut. Both were exiled.[223] But for his nephew that was not enough; he ordered the governor to cut his feet on arrival. As to his own brother Theodore, who insulted Martina, he was exiled to the island of Gozzo in Malta. The accomplices shared their fate.

Cruel Martina was no stranger to such atrocious acts for she incited her lover to punish anyone who dared to insult her. Her cruelty, deceit and wiles were compared by the people to Faustina, wife of Marcus Aurelius.[224]

The universal condemnation of the emperor reached a point where he took his seductress and hid with her in a palace outside the capital. The magistrates and the citizens pleaded with him to come back to the capital. They invoked

Lament for Jerusalem

the divinities in the churches and begged him to preside over the circus games but he refused, for he felt guilty and could not face the people and see the disgust on their faces. He wanted them to forget him and his shame. For feast days he delegated his sons to represent him – they returned in the evenings to console their unfortunate father.[225]

The joy that Martina gave him was at the expense of the respect and admiration that his people gave him before. Martina turned that into indifference and scorn. The army in Syria fighting to death and losing battles against the Persians came near to deserting him when they heard the news of his marriage and of his hiding with his seductress.[226]

Heraclius had to pay a heavy price for the languid siren Martina; for the whole establishment, the army, the people and some of his own imperial family could not stomach his marriage, nor his retreat to cover his shame.

Shame and guilt were foreign to Martina. She was obsessed by greed and grandeur, she could not let insults pass by – she nagged Heraclius until he punished those who slighted her, she accused his brother of having called her "the sin of the emperor" and had Heraclius exile him. This put people on their guard and so they kept their mouths shut. A close friend of Heraclius told him, "If it wasn't for this war and for poverty and disease that hit the capital, the people could have toppled you off the throne, but they are too weary and exhausted to revolt."

Martina gave her lover no peace; she was consumed by ambition and insisted that she must be crowned as empress with the full regalia and ceremony but Heraclius hesitated. He told her to look around and see the state in the capital, the news of the war was disastrous and the time was not

Two Sirens: Shirin and Martina

propitious for such a ceremony. Martina pouted. "I am your wife, not your concubine. Either I am empress or just one of your women around the palace. You crowned your daughter Eudokia and made her Augusta." Heraclius gave in to her wish and had her crowned empress by the Patriarch Sergius[227] at the Augusterion, the square facing St Sophia. She made him later give the title Augusta to her two daughters, Augustine and Martina for he could never say no to the siren who was pushing him to utter destruction.

Heraclius was aware of the dangerous situation but he was a devout religious man and the fact that he broke a basic rule in the Orthodox Church tormented him. He meditated and studied the stars – his nights were sleepless. How could he spend the rest of his life trying to live down the shame of his marriage, how could he ever regain his popularity and religious authority? One night he got away from the clutches of Martina and was gazing at the stars when an idea hit his weary head – he would conduct a religious war of Christianity against paganism, he would liberate Jerusalem and restore its precious relic: the piece of the cross. A sudden light shone upon his face. I will fight for the cross – a crusade. He then slowly and coldly began to set his plan in motion. He would leave the capital and make Armenia, the land of his people, his base.

The emperor was so excited he could not sleep. Tomorrow I will give the order for my son Constantine to replace me in the capital; he will rule with the help of the Patriarch – tomorrow I will leave Martina alone in Constantinople – tomorrow I will invent the crusade.

Heraclius won the war of the cross against the Persians but lost the Orient to the Arabs. He returned to the capital to occupy himself with the Western border and the barbarians. People never forgot his marriage but he was now an old broken man suffering from dropsy, a disease he judged was incurable – he was obliged every time he took water to put a block of wood on his stomach to prevent fluid from building up. He suffered from fainting. The horrible disease was considered by everybody as a punishment for the incestuous marriage he contracted with his niece, the siren that enchanted him.

---

221 Persian and Arabic sources claim that he was the son of Maria, daughter of the emperor Maurice
222 Nicephore, 2009, p. 3
223 Nicephore, p. 28 Michael the Syrian, Chronique, p. 49
224 Michael the Syrian, Chronique, p. 49
225 Michael the Syrian, Chronique, p. 350
226 Michael the Syrian, Chronique, p. 350
227 Theophane, the Chronicle, p.11

CHAPTER VIII

THE ARABIAN FACTOR IN THE WAR

A popular view of the part the Arabs played in the Great War is that they sat on the fence watching their neighbours, the two great empires, committing suicide in a long and protracted war; that when both were exhausted they jumped from the fence into the fray and conquered both empires. This is a simplistic, romantic version and utterly false, for in fact they were directly and indirectly involved throughout. At the beginning of the 7th century, the Arabs found themselves between a Christian Rome and a Zoroastrian Persia, fighting to death for lands the Arabs had settled in since ancient times – long before they became Persian or Roman territories.

Besides the two sedentary Arab kingdoms of Lakhm and Ghassan, marauding Bedouin tribes from the centre and north of the Arabian peninsula roamed the territory, raiding and pillaging – a fact of life which the two empires could not cope with. The two Arab kingdoms who allied themselves with the empires exercised some control over them.

The Great War offered a field day for these tribes by increasing opportunities for raids and incursions on both sides. But even when the war ended and Heraclius was

Lament for Jerusalem

negotiating the withdrawal of Persian troops with Shahrbaraz, they pillaged all around him.[228]

Other Arabs, the sedentary merchants of Mecca, were trading with both empires, heedless of war and occupation. Connection between Hidjaz and Syria was not suspended. Three major Arab groups in Hidjaz, Iraq and Syria were involved in the war as observers, sympathizers, antagonists and direct participants. The first group was in Hidjaz, which, although not in the orbit of the two powers, did have some Persian influence in Medina through the Lakhmids, and strong commercial ties with Syria, for Mecca was a caravan city, with its winter and summer caravans. Besides commerce, Hidjaz had cultural ties with fellow Arabs, Ghassan and Lakhm allies of Rome and Persia.

The Great War started when the prophet, with his few followers, was struggling with the unbelievers of Quraysh. These early Muslims sympathized with the Romans as people of the Book; Christians against the pagan fire-worshipers. They also had sympathy for Christians because of the welcome Christian Ethiopia afforded Muslim refugees who fled Mecca from the persecution of Quraysh in 615, during the Great War. This sympathy is reflected in the Surat Al Rum in the Qu'ran.

Surat Al Rùm[229]
1. Alif lam Mim
2. The Roman Empire has been defeated
3. In a land close by: But they, even after this defeat of theirs, will soon be victorious
4. Within a few years with Allah is the Decision. In the past and in the future On that day shall the believers rejoice

5. With the help of Allah He helps whom He will and He is exalted in Might most merciful
6. It is the promise of Allah. Never does Allah depart from His promise but most men understand not.

Pagan Quraysh rejoiced in the victory of the pagans of Persia, hoping that the movement of Islam would collapse at their persecution. They taunted the Muslims so aggressively that Abu Bakr, friend of the prophet and future Caliph, made a bet (before gambling was prohibited by Islam) with U'bay, a man from Quraysh, on the outcome of the Great War. He bet ten she-camels that the Romans would win the war in three years (he later changed the bet, wagering 100 she-camels that the Romans would win in nine years). U'bay did not live to see the Persian defeat, for he was killed by Muslims at U'hud and Abu Bakr won the 100 camels from his heirs. The prophet asked Abu Bakr to give the camels to charity.[230]

This early sympathy with the Romans faded during the long war. Merchants from Mecca saw the state of destruction in Roman towns and observed the antipathy of the Jacobite Syrians towards the Roman government – conditions propitious for the future Arab invasion, which began with the incursion at Mu'ta in 629, one year after the war ended.

The Muslim Arab army which conquered Palestine and Syria was assisted by the pockets of Arabs who had settled there and by deserters from the Roman Army who acted as guides and informers.

The second Arab group involved in the Great War were the Arabs of Iraq who were antagonists of Persia. The formidable army of the kingdom of Hira did not participate

Lament for Jerusalem

in the war because the kingdom was dissolved in 602, ending Arab rule in Iraq just before the Great War began. The liquidation of the Lakhmid kingdom aroused Arab wrath and resulted in the battle of Dhu Qar.

The date of the battle is not clear but according to Mas'udi it was 40 years after the birth of the prophet. This puts it in 610, in the midst of the Great War, when the Persians were attacking Syria[231] and losing the battle in Iraq. The Persian commander defeated by the Arabs was a friend of Parviz and was so important that he had nine seals of ruby and other precious stones.[232]

The only recorded participation of Arabs on the side of Persia was probably from a tribe that remained loyal. This participation was in Armenia at the beginning of the Roman counter-offensive in 622/623, when a scouting party of Heraclius met with a group of long-haired Saracans (not Lakhmids) who hoped to ambush the Romans. They were caught and brought to the chief who pardoned them.[233]

Of the Arabs of Iraq that took the war as an opportunity to attack Persia proper, the most famous leader was Muthana Ibn Haritha of the tribe of Shaiban who fought the Persians in the battle of Dhu Qar and who continued attacks when the war ended to throw the Persians out of Iraq. Muthana, a pagan Arab, implored the Muslim Caliph Omar to send an army from Hidjaz to join him in the invasion of Persia. The Caliph responded after much insistence from Muthana and asked him to convert, along with his tribe, to Islam. He sent him Khalid Ibn Al-Walid whom he recalled from the front in Syria. The Arab army from Hijaz, with the Arab tribes of Iraq, succeeded in throwing the Persians out of the country. The Persians understood too late their folly of antagonizing

The Arabian Factor in the War

the Arabs by ending the Arab rule and tried without success to conciliate them by reinstating the Lakhmid rule and putting a descendant on the throne. The Arabs of Iraq were set on conquering Persia. The non-participation of the Arabs of Iraq in the war was in the last analysis detrimental to the Empire of the Rising Sun, for these Arabs used their knowledge of Persian arms, their war tactics, the strategy they had acquired as former allies, and their zeal for the new faith, to conquer and subjugate Persia.

A third Arab group, the Ghassanids, participated actively and directly in the Great War alongside the Romans from beginning to end. This active involvement began in the reign of Phocas who murdered their arch enemy, Maurice. The advent of Phocas relieved the Ghassanids, for they were mistreated and distrusted by Maurice who exiled their king Nundir to Sicily, and his son N'uman to the capital. Phocas released their king from exile out of spite for the dead Maurice and wanted to count on the loyalty of the Ghassanids. The Ghassanids showed their gratitude by their participation in the imperial army from the very start of the war. The presence in the Persian army of the pretender, Theodosius, son of Maurice, whether true or fictitious, incensed the Ghassanids and added to their cry of vengeance.[234]

The war began in the provinces of Mesopotamia and Armenia. The Ghassanids participated in campaigns in both these areas,[235] besides carrying their own war into Persia proper through regular attacks and incursions all through the war. Their relationship with Phocas, however, began to sour because of his persecution of the Jacobites, a cult to which they belonged. Their alienation from Phocas reached a point which made them sympathize with the revolt of the Heraclii,

Lament for Jerusalem

and when Nicetas invaded Egypt they welcomed him as a deliverer and joined him in Egypt to fight Bonosus, the general of Phocas. On the defeat of Bonosus in Egypt, the Ghassanids quickly opted for the new emperor, Heraclius. A year later they joined Nicetas and Heraclius in the battle for the defence of Antioch. Upon defeat, they retreated with Nicetas to Egypt.

The invasion of Syria was in full swing when Nicetas rushed from Egypt with his army for an encounter with the Persians near Emessa, where a fierce battle took place. The sources are not clear whether it was a Roman victory or defeat, maybe a draw, since the Persians halted for two years (611-613) to regroup and reorganize.[236]

The attack on Syria was now resumed after the two year halt by the Persians; and again the Ghassanids rushed with Nicetas to defend their homeland. Damascus was occupied in 613 and the door to Palestina Secunda was now opened. A violent battle was fought in the domain of the Ghassanids who, together with the Imperial army, fought the last battle before the fall of Jerusalem. Nothing stood between the Persians and the Holy City; Ghassan land was left in desolation. Two pre-Islamic poets, Al-Nabigha and Hassan bin Thabet, who were habituates of the Ghassanid court, describe the wasted land and its barren desolation. For the Ghassanids the disaster was double; on the one hand losing their land and kingdom, and on the other, as Christians, failing to protect Jerusalem when they considered themselves custodians and protectors of its holy places.

Part of the Ghassanid army retreated again with Nicetas to Egypt and those who remained in the land after occupation carried the war to Persian territory[237] in frequent raids and incursions. When Egypt fell in 619 the Ghassanids retreated with Nicetas to the capital. Heraclius, while preparing for the counter-offensive, incorporated the Ghassanids into the new army he was organizing.[238] The Ghassanids acted as scouts for the army and accompanied Heraclius when he camped with 40,000 soldiers in the city of Ganzak where he sent his Saracen (Ghassanid) scouts for reconnaissance. The Arabs encountered the guard force of Parviz (Kisra II), massacred them, and brought the rest as captives to Heraclius. Parviz fled from Ganzak leaving his army but Heraclius pursued him, and slew some of the soldiers while the others fled.[239]

Heraclius acknowledged the important role the Ghassanids played in the war in his victory bulletin which announced his victory in Nineveh to the Senate, and which was read in St Sophia. He referred to their Christianity as "those who live within our Christ-loving state"[240] and how he sent them with part of his army to Persia after Nineveh to see how things stood between Siroé, the newly proclaimed king and his imprisoned father, Parviz.

The Muslim Arabs of Hidjaz, whose sympathy with the Romans eroded during the long war, had a deal with a very close neighbouring Roman territory to Hidjaz, Aila (Aqaba), an important port on the Red Sea. The Arabs neutralized it by an accord between the prophet and the Bishop of Aila, Yuhanna b. Ruba, in which the Arabs were to guarantee the safety of the inhabitants, as well as their ships and caravans, from raids and pillage by the Arab tribes, against the payment of 300 gold dinars by each non-Muslim adult, the use of the cisterns of Aila, and a free passage by land and sea.

Aila capitulated to the Arab demands because it was no longer protected by the X Roman Legion which was dispersed during the war and the limitans were absent because of lack of funds. To the Arabs, Aila opened the oriental door permanently for Sinai and the Negev and was a place of rest, food and water for their caravans.

Aila proved later a passage for the Arab army to Palestine. The Arab general Amr b. Al-As with 7,500 soldiers was ordered by Abu Bakr to proceed from there to the conquest of Palestine.[241]

The Arabs of Hijaz waited for a year after the war ended to send an expedition to a neighbouring Roman territory, Mu'ta near Karak. One version attributes it to the tradition (Hadith) for revenge against the Ghassanids for the murder of the envoys sent by the prophet to the emperor Heraclius.[242] The contingent was led by Zayd b. Haritha and was routed in a bloody defeat by the Ghassanids and the garrison south of the Red Sea. The Romans had grown used to border raids by the Arabs and did not view the Arab Muslim incursion at Mu'ta out of the ordinary. The emperor himself was familiar with those incursions, for when he was negotiating with Shahrbaraz, or celebrating victory over the Persians, they were pillaging around him.[243] The impact of the new Muslim faith on Arabia was partly ignored by the Romans, to the extent that some dismissed the new faith as a religious cult, a new heresy among many new cults that sprang from Christianity. Therefore they were not alarmed by the new Arab advances.

The Roman counter-offensive in 622 coincided with the prophet's move to Medina and the spread of Islam, but how aware Heraclius was of the power of the new faith and its danger for the empire is not evident – which is curious, as

The Arabian Factor in the War

Heraclius reigned during the life of the prophet and the Caliphs Abu Bakr and Omar b. Al-Khitab and two years into the reign of the Caliph Usman.[244]

The Arab conquest came on the heels of Roman victory. Only eight years separate victory from defeat, Nineveh from Yarmuk. Perhaps Heraclius was too confident but probably his energy had been spent on his counter-offensive, rendering his army enfeebled and exhausted. The Ghassanids fought in Yarmuk with other Arab tribes loyal to Rome, who pitted themselves against their fellow Arabs. But they and the Romans were defeated. Two years after Yarmuk, Jerusalem fell to the Arabs with some feeble resistance. Sophronius the Patriarch was repairing the destroyed monuments, his tears not yet dry after the sack of Jerusalem and his two lamentations on everybody's lips. Jerusalem capitulated to the Caliph Omar, who came from Hidjaz on the request of Sophronius. Once again, the city was not garrisoned, for the Roman army was spread over the eastern and western frontiers of the Empire. In the agreement with the Caliph, Sophronius insisted that the Arabs respect the clause in the decree of Heraclius which stated that Jews were prohibited to live within three miles of the city. He explained to the Caliph that the inhabitants were still traumatized by the massacre of 614 and feared another massacre by the Jews. The Ghassanid army retreated after Yarmuk with Heraclius to Anatolia – it was their third and last retreat. The first was from Antioch with Nicetas, the second from their homeland with the Roman army and the last retreat to Anatolia with Heraclius after Yarmuk. Some of the Ghassanids who stayed behind converted to Islam and others remained Christian. All, though, cooperated with the new Arab masters and fought

Lament for Jerusalem

their wars. They fought with Mu'awiyah, the governor of Syria and future Umayyad Caliph, against the Caliph Ali in the battle of Siffin. It is most probable that the Ghassanids returned to Orthodoxy under Heraclius for they suffered much as Jacobites (Monophysites), a cult they adopted under the emperor Anastius when they became allies of Rome.

The Muslim/Arab armies of the conquest benefited greatly from former Lakhmid and Ghassanid soldiers who joined the new army as converts. Their knowledge of arms, strategy and tactics was useful to the new force. Arab merchants, with their knowledge of Roman cities, acted as informers to the new army and some Arab tribes (former allies of Rome, angered by the non-payment of the tribute they were paid annually because of the financial ruin of the empire after the war) acted as guides and showed the Muslim/Arab force the route to Gaza and other towns in Palestine.[245] The Romaic Arabs (Romanized Arabs), settled in Syria and Palestinian towns since ancient times, were also of great help to their conquering fellow Arabs.

Heraclius, heartbroken, retreated with his army to the capital to dream of his Ekthesis, which was of no more use, for the unity between east and west, Orthodox and Jacobite, was blown to the wind as he lost his east, and his Jacobite subjects, who welcomed the Arabs. He realized that the Arab conquest was final and he did not resort to dynastic marriages with Arabs to redress the situation, as before with Turks and Persians. The emperor's obsession with conversion to Christianity was well known, but when the Patriarch of Alexandria, after the fall of Egypt, suggested to the emperor he give his unfortunate daughter Eudokia, or one of his two other daughters, in marriage to the Arab

Commander Amr b. al-As (the conqueror of Alexandria) with the possibility of converting him to Christianity, Heraclius was furious at the suggestion. He called the Patriarch an enemy of Christian religion and accused him of delivering Alexandria to the Arabs, threatening to kill him or put him in the hands of the prefect.

Heraclius' dream of a new, unified empire based on the Asiatic provinces evaporated and his only consolation was to return to the study of the stars. But only for a short time, for he had a firm belief, in keeping with his generation, that at this period the world will end.

228 L. Bréhier, Le Monde, p. 58, Shahid, 6th cent., vol. 2, 2002, p. 32, Nicephore, 2009, p. 23
229 Abdullah Yusuf Ali, The Holy Qur'an Text, translation and commentary Amana Corporation 1989, Brentwood, Maryland, USA, pp. 1008, 1009
230 Muhie Al-Din, Shiek Zandek in the Tafsir of Al-Bardoir, 1981
231 Mas'udi, Muruj, vol. 1, p. 289
232 Mas'udi, Muruj, vol. 1, p. 285
233 Shahid, 6th century, p. 643
234 Shahid, 6th century, vol. 1, 1995, p. 622
235 Shahid op. cit
236 Shahid, 1995, p. 635
237 Ekkebus, Heraclius, p. 108
238 Shahid, 1995, p. 645
239 Shahid, 1995, p. 641, quotes Theophaness, Chronographie, p. 307
240 Shahid, op. cit. p. 642
241 Dauphin, C., La Palestine, vol. II, 1998, pp. 341, 362
242 Dauphin, op. cit. p. 961
243 Nicephore, 2009, p. 23
244 Mas'udi Al-Tabih, 1893, p. 157
245 Cameron, The Mediterranean, 1993, p. 189

Epilogue

For reasons beyond our limited understanding Jerusalem has always been a sanctuary – its name, Ur-Salem (City of Peace) indicates a Mesopotamian connection followed by Canaanites from whom it was conquered by the Hebrews. Constantine and Helena made it a centre of Christianity for the East Roman Empire, but the Jerusalem that aroused awe and veneration in the human heart had another face that awakened hate and violent passions, leading ultimately to massive bloodshed.

The celestial city suffered two crusades in the 7th and 11th centuries with consequences that stretch to our present day. The first crusade, the subject of this brief study, was characterized by slaughter, exile and depopulation; the second by a massacre which filled the streets with blood. Both indirectly planted the seeds for the present thorny relationship between Arabs and Persians and the Arab-Israeli conflict.

The international community, aware of the dangers of the Arab-Israeli conflict, with its ingredients of fanatic, passionate hate arising out of those two early crusades, and haunted by fear of the catastrophic results of further bloodshed in and around Jerusalem if the conflict continues,

Lament for Jerusalem

is trying to bring about a just peace for Jerusalem. Peace will resurrect the divided and wounded city, forming a whole metropolis of fellowship and brotherhood, and it will enable the city to regain its legendary role as centre of our universe.

BIBLIOGRAPHY

Abgarian – Remarques sur l'Histoire de Sébéos in *Revue d'études arméniennes*, 19654. Fragment de Sébéos in Armenien History, 1984

Al-Shabi, Felix – The Feast of the Cross.
Website http:kaldaya.article5.2008

Antiochus Strategos – Capture of Jerusalem by the Persians in AD 614 trans. C. Conybeare in *English Historical Review 25*, 1914
Website: www.ccehorg/cel/christianclassicsethical/library

Avi-Yonah – *The Jews of Palestine from the Bar Koba war to the Arab Conquest*, Oxford, 1976

Ben Abrahamson and Joseph Katz – *The Persian Conquest of Jerusalem in 614 compared with Islamic conquest of AD 638* (created with PdF)

Bendall – The Byzantine Coinage of the mint of Jerusalem, *Revue numismatique*, vol. 6, n° 159, 2003
Website: http:www.persee.fr

Bréhier, Louis – *Le monde byzantine: vie et mort de Byzance*, Paris, 1946

Cameron, Averil – *The Mediterranean World in Late Antiquity*, London, 1993

Dagron et Deroche – Juifs et Chrétiens, dans L'Orient du VIIe siècle in *Travaux et Mémoires II*, 1991

Dauphin, Claudine – La Palestine byzantine, vol. II, Bar International Series 726, Oxford, 1998

Lament for Jerusalem

Delgado, Martinez – Les versions arabes de la destruction de Jérusalem par les perses in *Revista de Ciencias de religiones*, ISN 135-4712 N° 11, 2006
Website : http://dialnet.unirioja/servlet/articulo

Dom. H. Leclerq – (trad. Et publiés) Les Martyres, Tome IV, Juif, Sarrasins, Iconoclastes, Paris, 1905
Website : http :www.abbayestbenoit_ch/martyrs_001 htmtt toc 90636078

Ekkebus, B. – Heraclius and the Evolution of Byzantine strategy in constructing the past, vol. 10:issue/1/11, article II, Illinois, USA 2009
Website http/digitalcommons.iwu/edu/constructing/vol.10.iss

Eutychius – Sa'id ibn Batriq Annalen (trans) des annals des l'oriens chistones, tome 65, 1981 (trad. Cheik bard de Vaux)

Ferdowsi – The Shah Nameh, Calcutta, 1829

Frolow, A. – La déviation de la 4e croisade versa Constantinople et les guerres persanes d'Héraclius, *Revue de l'Histoire des religions*, vol. 17, n° 1, 1955

Garitte – La prise de Jérusalem par les Perses en 614, *Corpus Scriptorum Christenorum Orientalium*, vols. 202-203, 1973

Goubert, S.T. – Byzance avant l'Islam, Tome I, Paris, 1951

Horowitz, Elliot – The vengeance of the Jews was stronger than their avarice, modern Historians and the Persian Conquest of Jerusalem in 614, in Social Studies, new series, vol. 4, n° 2, 1998
Website: http:www.jistot.org/14467519

Iorga, N. – Histoire de la vie byzantine empire et civilisation, Bucarest, 2004

Bibliography

Website : http :www.undmc.no/classica/broga/cuptih.htm

Jewish Encylopedia, New York, 1901-1906 – entries on Khosroes II and Bahran Chubain.
Website: http/www/jewishencyclopedia.com.view_friendly/jsp

La vraie voix et les expéditions d'Héraclius en Perse, Syria, vol. 31, n° 3, 1954
Website : http :iwow.persie.fr

Mango, Cyril – Deux études sur Byzance et la Perse Sassanide dans Travaux et Mémoires, Tome 9, 1985

Mazar, Benjamin – *The Mountain of the Lord*, New York, 1975

Michael the Syrian – Chronique, dans Journal asiatique et cahiers numérisée par Marc Szwajcer, 1865
Website: remacle.org/bloodwolf/historiens/michelesyrien/table.htm

Mozilla Skin – Nehemia ben Hushiel and the Jewish Crusade 1962
Website: http://www.alnehemiah 1962

Nicephore – Patriarche de Constantinople Histoire de l'empereur Héraclius, (trad.) Cousin, Tome III, Paris, 2009 (Edition 1685) MDCLXXXV

Prapeyron, Ludovic – *L'empereur Héraclius et l'empire Byzantin du VII siècle*, Paris, 1869

Rivkah Duker Fishnan – Perspectives. The Seventh Century Christian Obsession with the Jews, in *Jewish Political Studies*, Review 17, n° 4, 2005

Sébéos – *Histoire d'Héraclius* (trans. Frédéric Macler), Paris 1906

Shahid, Irfan – *The Iranian Factor in Byzantium during the reign of*

Lament for Jerusalem

Heraclius, Dumbarton Oaks Papers, vol. 26, 1972. Website: http://www.jstor.org/stable/1291324
Byzantium and The Arabs in the Sixth Century, vol. 1, part 1, 2. Dumbarton Oaks, Washington DC, 1995

Shamir, Israel – *614, après Jesus Christ the Genocide of Mamilla in Palestine*, 2009
Website: www.alterinfo.net/pye.http/Shamirmediamonitors.net

Shick, R. – *The Christian Communities of Palestine from Byzantine to Islamic rule*, Princeton, 1995
Christians in Jerusalem in early 7th century A.D. in *Patterns of the Past Prospects for the Future, the Christian Heritage in the Holy Land*, ed. Thomas Hummet and Kevork Hintlian, London, 1999

Sophronius – Anacreontica, vol. VIII, (trans.) Marcellus Gigante, Rome 1957

Sophronius – La prise de Jerusalem par les Perses, 614 dans Revue de l'Orient Christian numérisée par Marc Swajeer, n° 1, 4, Paris, 1897
Website : remacle.org/bloodwolf/eglise/sophronicus/jerusalem

Sophronius – First Elegy dans La prise de Jérusalem par les Perses, Revue de l'Orient chrétien, Paris, 1897.
Website http :remacle /org/bloodwolf/eglise/origene/table/htm, Bibliothèque nationale cabinet des titres Latin, n° 3282, Ch XVI, folio, 26, 27

Stratos – *Byzantium in the 7th century*, Amsterdam, 1968

The Cambridge History of Iran vol. 3, part 1, Byzantium and the Sassanians, Cambridge, 1983

The Holy Qur'an (translation and commentary by Abullah Y. Ali (revised edition) Brentwood, Maryland, USA, 1989

Bibliography

Theophanes – *The Confessor, The Chronicle. Byzantine and Near Eastern History*, Oxford, 1997
Chronographia (trans.) Turtledove, Philadelphia, 1982

Ubierna, Pablo – Recherches sur l'apocalyptique Syriaque et Byzantine au VII siècle in *Bulletin du Centre d'études médiévales d'Auxerre*, n° 21, 2009

Zuckerman, Constantin – La petite Augusta et la Turc Epiphania-Eudocie sur les monnaies d'Heraclius dans Revue numismatique, vol. 6, n° 150, 1995
Website : www.persee.fr/web/revues/home/prescri

ARABIC SOURCES

1. Al-Badawi, Anwar Al Tanzil, Beirut, 1996
2. Al-Thàlabi, Tafsir, Beirut
3. Al-Dimaski, Ismail, Tafsir Al Qu'ran, Beirut, 1969
4. Al-Tabari, Jami Al-Baron, Beirut, 1995
5. Al-Zamakhsheri, Al-Kashaf, Beirut, 1995
6. Ibn-Al-Athir, Al-Kamel fi Al-Tarikh, Beirut,1982
7. Ibn Al-Juzi, Al-Munatham, Beirut, 1992
8. Al-Mas'udi, Muruj Al Thahab, Beirut, 1997
9. Al-Mas'udi, Kitab Al-Aanbih wa Il-Ishraf, Leiden, 1893
10. Jawad, Ali, Al-Mufesal Fi Tarikh Al-Arab Qabl Al-Islam, 2nd ed., Baghdad, 1993
11. Al Hamaoui, Mujum Al-Balden, Beirut, 1995
12. Al Na'wari, Nichayat Al-Arab fi Funun Al-Adab, Beirut, 2004
13. Ibn-Kathir, Al-Bidaya, wa Al-Nihaya, Damascus
14. Al-Tabari, Tarikh Al-Rusul wa Al-Muluk, Beirut, 2004
15. Ibn Khaldun Kitab Al-Ibir wa Diwan al Mubtada wa al-Khabar, Beirut
16. Al Dianuri, Al Akhbar Al-Thwal, Cairo, 1960
17. Ibn Maskawayh, vol. 1